# GOD SPEAKS
## here and now

### A Guide for Living

Conversations with the
Source of All Knowing

Dorit and Michael Har
Ruth Seagull

Sunstar
PUBLISHING LTD.

God Speaks Here and Now
A Guide for Living
Conversations with the Source of All Knowing
© United States Copyright, 1998
Dorit Har
Sunstar Publishing, Ltd.
204 South 20th Street
Fairfield, Iowa 52556

Cover & Text Design: Amanda Collett

Library of Congress Catalog Card Number: 98-061338
ISBN: 1-887472-54-1

Readers interested in obtaining further information on the subject matter of this book are invited to correspond with
The Secretary, Sunstar Publishing, Ltd.
204 South 20th Street, Fairfield, Iowa 52556
More Sunstar Books at www.newagepage.com

# Dedication

*I dedicate this book to the spirit of my father, Shlomo Frank (Frenkel) who came to Earth to teach joy and unconditional love under any circumstances. My father who travels the worlds in the service of God, who never left me and never will, because we are one in our desire to unite with God. My father has shown me greatness in all situations and has been present, like a guardian angel at my right, supporting and guiding every step of my growth. With infinite kindness and gentleness he makes his presence known, and guides me to fully live in truth and love.*

# Acknowledgments

I would like to thank divine guidance for directing me in my spiritual pursuit, patiently allowing me to explore and play the surface, lovingly leading me Home. Thank You, God, for entrusting this special message into our hands and making it all happen.

My gratitude to the Teachers who gave me the tools to deepen my understanding, expand my awareness and experience the transcendent. My deep love and appreciation to the Masters of various religions and paths, who inspire me on my journey.

My love to my mother who taught me to always look forward, who intuitively trusted in me and allowed me to venture forth. Love and thanks to my husband, Michael, who courageously chose to take the first steps of our spiritual journey. He has been sharing himself so devotedly, and no matter what, maintained commitment to reach balance and harmony. Love for my children, Lael and Matan, for being my best friends and teachers, and for recognizing the importance of the task, giving up "play time."

My deepest gratitude to Ruth Seagull for becoming my endeared friend and buddy in this journey for more. Thank you for believing in me and making this book possible with endless love, determination and support.

My very special thanks to Chari Albino, Jan Bocskay, Rifka Kreiter, John Matozzi, Bill and Brenda Pollak, Naomi Singer, Bob Snyder and Gloria Wendroff for reading the first draft, contributing their insights and believing that there is a book in it. Thanks also to our first editor, Katharine Hanna, for her integrity, wonderful work and contribution.

From the bottom of my heart, love and thanks to all the wonderful people who came to me for spiritual consultations and trusted in my new ability, trusted in God, and opened their heart to the possibilities which lie beyond the mind.

Lastly, my deepest gratitude to my dear friend for sharing with me her truth and directing me to this magic journey.

"Talking with God is a definite fact. In India I have been in the presence of saints while they were talking with the Heavenly Father. And all of you, also, may communicate with Him; not a one-sided conversation, but a real talk wherein you speak to God and He responds. Everyone can talk to the Lord, of course. But I am discussing today how we may persuade Him to reply to us... Why should we doubt? The scriptures of the world abound in descriptions of talks between God and man. (page 7.)

"We should speak to the Divine Spirit with confidence and with a feeling of closeness, as to a father or a mother. Our relationship with God should be one of unconditional love. More than in any other relationship we may rightfully and naturally demand a reply from Spirit in Its aspect as the Divine Mother. God is constrained to answer such an appeal; for the essence of a mother is love and forgiveness of her child, no matter how great a sinner he may be.

"And the demand for the Lord's reply should be strong; a half-believing prayer is not sufficient. If you make up your mind: 'He is going to talk with me'; if you refuse to believe differently, regardless of how many years He has not answered you; if you go on trusting Him, one day He will respond. (pages 8,9.)

"God also talks to man through his intuition. If you learn how to listen to the Cosmic Vibration it is easier to hear His voice. But even if you just pray to God through the cosmic ether, if your will is strong enough, the ether will respond with His voice. He is ever talking to you, saying: 'Call Me, speak unto Me from the depth of your heart, from the core of your being, from the very depth of your soul, persistently, majestically, determinedly, with a firm resolve in your heart that you will go on seeking Me, no matter how many time I do not answer. If you unceasingly whisper in your heart to Me, 'O my silent Beloved, speak to me,' I will come to you, My devotee.'

"If once you can get that response you will never feel separated from Him again. The Divine experience will always remain with you. But that 'once' is difficult because the heart and mind are not convinced; doubt creeps in because of our previous materialistic beliefs.

"Think of all the things that came to me today and that I have told you. You should never again doubt that God will respond to you, if you are constant and persistent in your demands." (pages 33-35.)

from *How You Can Talk With God*
by Paramahansa Yogananda

# Table of Contents

## Introduction:

Another book about God? No, this time it is a book *from* God. God speaks to you as He speaks to me and to everyone who believes it's possible. This idea was presented to me by a dear friend who had a near death experience. After recovering, she discovered a new ability within herself--she could converse with God. I was fascinated, but thought it couldn't happen to me. While my mind was reasoning "impossible," my heart kept on yearning and trusting that it was possible. Whether for you this possibility is a fiction or nonfiction, read this book with an open mind and let your heart decide.

On June 25th, 1995, clearly and beyond doubt, I heard the 'voice' of God in my heart saying, "Dear Dorit, there is much love for you. It's all going to happen..." The 'voice' was an inner knowing that formed into words. I knew, body and soul, mind and heart, that this indeed was the 'voice' of God. A tremendous wave of joy and relief washed over me. I was coming Home. I burst into joyful laughter.

A few months later, what had started as hesitant sessions of questions and answers had turned into a flow of messages. At first what I received was in poetic Hebrew, my mother tongue. Since I had a desire to share it with my friends here, I was given the choice to use any language, so I decided on English. I spoke out the words of God while Michael, my husband, asked questions, first his own and then others'. This process has been blissful, and effortless and the contribution it makes to our lives and others' lives is tremendous. Now, after many 'voice hours' and experiences of healing, grace and guidance--my own and those of 'my' listeners and readers--I know, beyond any doubt, that what seemed impossible is possible. We have formed a wonderful friendship with the Source of All Knowing, an intimate relationship that's always loving, encouraging and never judging. The inner growth, understanding, compassion, love, joy, purification, sense of wonder that were added to our lives are priceless. Life indeed is a celebration!

From the beginning of this 'adventure' it was made clear that this knowledge was to be shared with the public in the form of a book, and that the words of God would bring healing to many. A great deal of information on various topics came through and we wondered how it could be organized into sequential chapters. God's response was,

"Decisions are a good thing to make only when they come easily. The true nature of decisions is acting on what the universe has already been deciding for you and then it naturally flows. Your insight into the unfolding of the book will come naturally. You see, the book is already written. It's now up to you to rewrite it in the physical."

On August 24, 1996, God added, "I ask for a 30 day commitment. I am taking your hands now, both of you, and We are embarking on a new journey, in which together We will experience the exhilaration, and the outcome will be the book. The purpose of the book is to convey the message that God is here and now, to leave the readers with the feeling that God jumps out of the book into their lives; that they cannot turn around and not 'see' God any more. God is a tangible force in everyday life. God is what moves you. God is the essence of your lives, always was and always will be."

Of course, we could hardly refuse such an offer! As was suggested, we prioritized our time, and with great excitement and determination embarked on the journey. We were not the only ones. From the beginning our friend Ruth Seagull shared with us the exhilaration of new discoveries and followed the process closely. The reason for our mutual attraction became very clear when God said to Ruth,

"You are an essential leg in this four-legged table, an instrument in the awakening to the Truth. Therefore, I orchestrated all the circumstances for the three of you to work together. This is something you agreed to do together."

In the next 30 days Michael and I received the messages and taped them while Ruth transcribed them. Together, we compiled all the material. Indeed, we worked as a team through all the stages of bringing this book to life.

Well, I have to admit that there were moments when old doubts crept in. Old ideas about God and His unavailability to ordinary people like me surfaced in my mind more than once. Bit by bit these deeply rooted concepts about who can hear God and the prerequisites for receiving divine wisdom were dissolved. A new reality dawned, a reality of infinite expansion and intimacy with God.

When we asked why so many people are now experiencing a shift in awareness, the answer came, "New waves of energy are coming forth from the Source. Universes are colliding. The enormous, massive creation is shifting now at an ever increasing speed. And although human beings are an integral part of this process, they can easily find themselves ground in the gears of this massive shift. Attunement is essential for the shift to happen in the most 'pleasant' way for you. This is somewhat hard to explain since the blind cannot see, but even the blind can see with their inner eyes. Those who choose not to see will not survive the experience. Those who attune themselves and choose to see with their inner eyes will be able to ride the new waves. The best shortcut I can offer you is: cultivate a burning desire in your heart to be one with Me."

Then God said to Michael, "You and Dorit are messengers, two among many. My ways are infinite. There are many doors, there are many keys." We realized that God speaks to everyone and we don't need to deserve it. We are loved for who we are, here and now.

What helped to 'convince' me even more were experiences that were interlaced in the process of receiving the messages, given to me like a gift, with infinite patience and compassion. I received a taste of the vastness and the different energies that were discussed. Words like energy, love, light and truth came alive. My heart accelerated and excitement sent shivers of bliss to every cell of my body. Sometimes I felt like a happy, shining particle of love melting into a vast golden light inside my heart. My heart would expand and expand until I felt so enormous that there was no limit to me. These were my personal experiences, but of course God speaks to us in infinite ways.

Throughout this book God talks to us with words. The words are my choice, reflecting my vocabulary and capacity to express inner knowing. When once I asked how He talks to me, God said, "Words that come from Silence contain the Silence. When the words come out of your mouth, it is the end of a process which begins with pulses of energy that come from Me, God, or what you call God. These vibrations travel through the inner worlds, contact your soul and continue to your higher energy centers, those that are above your head. Through these energy centers the vibrations pour down to your heart. In your heart you receive the knowing, which you then translate into words. That's why I say that I reside in the Heart."

In going over and over this book while we prepared it for publication, we discovered new wisdom each time, new understandings to be integrated into our lives. We discussed it, even argued over it, in our effort to be clearer in our own knowing. So, even if you find the words you read don't quite make sense and the message is not clear to you, stay with it. Read the book more than once. Let it become your best friend. Share it with a friend. Bit by bit you will find the book working its magic in your life. With God's help, you will become your own best teacher, letting the book's truth touch your heart and change your life, here and now.

Quoting God's words, I would like to invite you to join the journey,

*"Be beautiful as you are*
*Be wonderful as you are*
*Be light as you are*
*Be a flower as you are*
*Be loving as you are and*
*Be and Be, and take Me with you all the way."*

Dorit Har
Fairfield, Iowa
January 1997

# A Personal Story

*By Bob Snyder*

Ever since I learned that I have cancer, I've known that old 'stuff' didn't work. Old behavior patterns didn't bring me happiness. Old concepts didn't bring me joy; and certainly, old belief systems didn't bring me peace. Intuitively I knew there must be a change to a new realization of life, a realization that is in perfect harmony with who I really am, a new orientation for living.

After I had my colon resectioned, I endured 43 weeks of chemotherapy only to find it hadn't worked. The cancer had spread to my liver and was so massive that it was inoperable. My weight dropped from 195 to 120 pounds and my energy was almost depleted. Imagine the fullness, the wholeness I felt when I was given, directly from All Intelligence the new orientation for living that I so desperately needed. Let me share with you the wonder of what God told me through Dorit Har,

"Dear Bob, I do understand the anxiety you are in right now. Your mind says 'ease,' but the rest of you is experiencing anxiety. I would like you to let go and trust that every detail of it will be just as perfect as you want it to be and ease will be your main resource. It is quite easy to do. When you lie in your bed or sit in the car, go over every part of your body, repeating the word ease and handing it over to Me. So your offering will be truly body and soul."

Please notice the utter simplicity of this subtle but powerful technique. "Bob, I want you to understand that you are almost on track. Ease is the link between awareness and physicality. 'Ease' is another word for introducing nonphysical to physical, bringing Me to every particle of your body. The "almost" part is that you are still holding the belief that there is some kind of God that sits in your heart, but it is more than that. *It* is in every cell of your body where you allow *It* to be. And when you allow *It* to be there, there is no body."

I asked: What is *It?*

"The awareness of God as being you."

Further, I was told: Most human beings leave this dimension without gaining the awareness of God being one with them. There are rare cases, rare situations, where people accomplish this oneness while in the physical body. Everyone accomplishes it when he comes Home. Truly it doesn't matter, the intent is what matters. What you want to accomplish is having the right intention, living in the now as if the oneness had already happened. And here I am referring to the will. Willing something means living it as if it had already happened. As long as the desire remains as a wish, the job is unfinished. When I say that human beings have free choice, it is this most powerful part that people forget. The free choice is in the ability to *will* your journey, to shorten it or lengthen it at your will. That's the free choice that you have. Your work now is to bring this understanding from your head to your heart, reverberating it in each cell of your body as if it had already experienced everything you wanted to experience. Then the shift will happen."

After receiving this profound knowledge, it was relatively easy to drop old behavior patterns and beliefs one by one. The next instruction brought with it the most joy I have ever known.

"I would like you to regard your future as a time, short or long, in which you prepare for vacation. Before you go on vacation, remember to pay your bills, take care of business, maintain what needs to be maintained, ask forgiveness from whomever you need to ask forgiveness, and then close what needs to be closed."

A simple clearing out of my life, no less!

"And you do it all with joy because you know you are going on vacation in a beautiful place. This is how I want you to regard your life, every moment of it. Experience the Now because every moment has a purpose. No one thing is more important than another. Everything is important. While you prepare for your vacation make sure you don't leave anything unfinished. All the dreams you had, fulfill them, or let them go. If you want to go on vacation on Earth, go ahead. When you prepare this closure, go over your 'files,' make sure there is no unfinished business."

For me, it was truly knowing that all is well. When expressing my desire to share this knowledge with others, God said,

"Bob, your only responsibility is to Be, and by Being, the love you experience will give a thousand times more than any word or explanation you give, because you teach by example. When your family sees you, Bob, sick with cancer, yet overflowing with joy, they will experience something they have never experienced before. So you see how your responsibility for your own Being is also your responsibility for the world."

This was the first time I felt I had the ability to love unconditionally and understood the oneness of my responsibility to myself and my brothers. I felt that this was quite a blessing.

Since I made this new orientation mine, I have thrived! I immediately felt better and my weight went back up to 150 pounds, my optimal weight. I receive no treatment, take no medicine and have been pain-free. Although I am technically still a cancer patient, I am patient with myself, patient with my life and patient with my illness. My doctor, who is the head of the oncology department at a near-by hospital, sees me every three months. During my last appointment, after examining me physically he paused a moment, looked me directly in the eye and quietly asked: "What are you doing, Bob?" So I looked him directly in the eye and quietly told him what I have shared with you. I encourage you to apply the knowledge offered in this book. It could change your life. It changed mine.

> Bob Snyder
> Endicott, N.Y
> December, 1996

During the last year Bob Snyder continued reaching out to God, deepening his realization and receiving Divine Guidance and Love. On December 5th, 1997, Bob made his transition into a different dimension with a smile on his face. He was ready for his new beginning.

In our last phone conversation, a few hours before Bob slipped into comma, he said:

"I want to say thank you to our Heavenly Father. Thank you right now for everything that He has given me and thank you for the opportunity to say, thank you.

I am so here, I am so here, I am so here! I am so awake, I am so awake, I am so awake!"

**Life is Eternal.**

December, 1997

A Note:

♦ **Starting with the prologue all text are God's words, except the questions which appear in *italic* letters.**

♦ Both genders are always included whether 'he' or 'she' is used.

♦ Throughout the book there are capitalization inconsistencies. However, within chapters consistency is maintained except to indicate subtle differences in meaning.

♦ Reference is made to one universal Law which has many different names.

♦ We decided to capitalize only the word Law to convey the idea that all universal laws are one.

♦ Messages from different dates may be combined in one chapter.

## Prologue

**Dear Children of the Light,**

We have come together today for you to hear the latest news.
God is here and now, always was, always will be in the now.
Open yourself to this truth, let it become a fundamental element in your life.
Bring God to your being, bring God to your living.
Bring God to every aspect of your life so you can Live.
God is the force which moves you and the world around you.
Give this force its rightful share in your awareness and watch the progress, watch the change, watch the joy.

The book I am placing in your hands today is a milestone in your long journey.
It is as personal as it can be.
Read it, my dear one, with an open mind and an open heart and attune yourself to My call.
Words are words, but the vibration that created them is eternal.
Attune yourself to this vibration.
Resonate with it.

I am inviting you to first read the book in an orderly unfoldment of truth. Make sure to read the first chapters which lay the foundation for the understanding of this truth--the hereness and nowness of God's force in your life. Then you may open the book wherever you want--the resonance is one. But however you choose to read the book, remember that truth is perceived with your whole being. While you keep your discriminative mind intact, trying to grasp meaning intellectually, maintain an innocent, trusting attitude and allow the truth to resonate in both your mind and your heart.

# 1

## Threshold to Infinity

Go within, go within now and always. "Within" feels like a physical location. You start by focusing your mind in the place inside you that is the seat of your soul, your heart. You focus your faculties into your heart. This is a way of bringing awareness of your body, your thoughts, your emotions, everything about you, into one point, your heart. When you go within, you depart from the world of your senses, from your outer reality and you are drawn to a different world, a different awareness, which is also you, which is more of you. This place that is more of you is your connection to the Absolute, your connection to the Source, where you were thought of and from which you were drawn into manifestation. By going within you train yourself and the energies that surround you to focus. Once you are trained in this one-pointedness, this one focal point becomes an opening, a threshold to infinite awareness. This is your door. In order to reach this door and to open it, you need to bring all of your faculties into this one place and feel it pulsate, feel it as real.

When you focus your faculties into one point in you--your heart-- you draw knowledge from there spontaneously, naturally, all day long. This is called living by the Law. And if people say, "How? We don't understand, how can we do it, what does it mean? My heart is just a beating organ," the answer is: quiet, quiet, quiet your mind, close your windows, shut your door, turn off the light, turn off the radio, turn off the TV, and listen. "I don't 'hear' anything?" That's probably what most people will say. Listen even more carefully, try again, try again, until you 'hear.' This you must do on a regular basis.

Imagine a funnel, in which the rim is wide. You are on the rim and when you want to go inside, you turn away from the outside and go to a narrower and deeper place that leads you to a very, very focused end that opens to infinity. And that infinity is where who you are was created and where you came from. It is where the very thought that thought you was created and then was motioned through the funnel to the outside rim, which is your physical world. If the very thought that created you came from within, this 'place' must be the origin of all that you know and all that you are.

So, if your inner awareness is curious enough to ask, "Who am I?" it is naturally drawn to the Source. Since you came from there you can go back there and understand who you are. You can find the balance point between the out and the in, the whole and the parts. You can walk on the outside surface while at the same time being connected to the point in the funnel which opens to infinity.

You hear the words 'go within' in many variations. Going within is like saying, "trust in God," or, "be in the flow," or, "peace, harmony, amen." 'Within' suggests the creative intelligence that underlies who you are, the source of everything. It also suggests the journey, the flow, the moving forward. It's always moving, moving. Where does it go? It goes to infinity in order to come back again. As was said, "Curving back upon myself I create again and again."[*]

*I assume that You are talking about meditation as one way to go within. What kind of meditation is best?*

No particular format is essential. Meditation is essential. At a set time, you 'close everything,' and your attention is drawn only to whatever you associate with 'within'--a name of God, a beautiful vision, a mantra--whatever works best to quiet the mind and withdraw from outside activity. This is essential not only for relaxation and rejuvenation, but also to instantly reach the door that opens to infinity. When you go through this funnel, by self-discipline, by mastering of time and space, you transcend the funnel bit by bit. You train your being to transcend it. This is the importance of meditation. Whatever form of meditation you choose

---

[*] Bhagavad Gitah, (9;8)

that brings you closer to this goal--finding yourself less scattered, finding yourself reaching the threshold, having glimpses of infinity--this is what you want.

In addition, imagine that in your heart there is an invisible kingdom. In this kingdom you are the ruler. You can set your own rules, your own standard of truth, your own reality, and your own beliefs. The wider this invisible kingdom of yours becomes, the more it will reflect on your visible world. The brighter and happier your inner kingdom becomes, the brighter and happier your external world will be. It's like a little game you can play and there are no limitations! This kingdom with its palaces won't cost you at all! And oh, how magnificent it can become, how generous, kind, loving and beautiful it can become! And with such a kingdom in your heart, what more would you want? With such a kingdom in your heart, you are the richest person in the world!

All physical manifestations originate in the heart at some point in time. Just as you know for sure that the sun always comes up, so you know for sure that anything can exist if you allow it, if you let it be projected as a pure thought, before you involve the outer faculties of your being. You see, this is like centrifugal movement of energy. Whatever starts to vibrate or rotate in the center, the heart, will eventually find its place on outer circles of this movement. Just as you know that the sun will come up, so you know that what manifests on the outer rim of this energy circle, originated in the center. Nothing comes to be without moving in this vibrational circle, originating as pure thought and ending up as "desire come true." But if you desire on the outer circle, moving about on the rim, pushing your way through and manipulating, then it is useless.

So, what do you learn from this? You learn that the best place to be is in your heart, wandering in the beautiful garden of your palace, living your reality in full trust and oneness. Then, there is no question of being impatient, feeling stuck, doubting, needing help, because in the palace you are fully taken care of. Everything is provided at the right time and the right place. Isn't it comforting to know that? And yet you choose to worry. You choose to wander outside the gate of this beautiful palace, asking, "Where is the palace? Does it exist?" And I keep on telling you, "Come back, come back. Where are you going? It is so beautiful here." The God who 'sits on the throne and rules the hosts' is in your heart.

April 20, 1996
August 24, 1996

## 2

## Journey In and Out

Good morning. Take a deep breath and join Me. We are embarking on a new journey, a journey to infinity. Yes, the objects around you seem steadfast. Everything seems the same--the objects outside, the furniture arranged around you. But nothing is really the same. Every moment everything is changing, and you are sitting in an invisible chariot, racing forward. While you are on the move, you do numerous things simultaneously. While you're on the go, you radiate light, send feelings of love, do what needs to be done, and absorb what needs to be absorbed. You never stop because what awaits you is even more blissful than what you leave behind. In this journey you join hands with those who move forward with you. You call to them, "Come, join us," and many do. This is a most beautiful, delightful parade. This is your life--constant flow. You are the conscious, blissful particles of the universe, twirling, somersaulting, moving forward in this infinite stream. So whenever you find yourself out of this stream, you know you don't belong out there.

Remember, the stability and comforting order around you are really just an illusory frame. True freedom finds balance within, it doesn't need an anchor. It's an infinite relationship of like attracts like. In this attraction, freedom finds balance. The structure of an atom reveals this true nature of life. The perfect balance of attraction and non-attraction among the subatomic particles, and the eternal motion and balance within this structure, reveal the Law of life. It is always moving toward harmony, bliss, peace and balance.

Your only stronghold, your only real anchor, is Me. The essence of these words is that when you put your trust in Me totally, peace and harmony are created in you, since you attune yourself with the underlying structure of the universe. Acceptance, surrender and trust excite you to seek perfect life, free of sorrows, free of disharmony, attracting only what is good. Any other balance you seek--gravity, a friend, a mate, or a beautiful home--is an illusion. They are all like beautiful scenery that you see while you move forward in your journey.

You are a blissful, free being on the journey for more, more expansion, more progress, more life, but when you introduce doubt, it is like pressing on the brakes. Doubt slows you down. Doubt is a creation of your mind. There is no doubt in the feeling of love. There is no doubt in the experience of bliss. There is no doubt in the awareness of harmony.

Doubt, according to the Law, like attracts like, will increase and multiply, attracting more of its kind. When doubt arises, acknowledge it as the creation of the mind. Use your mind, which brought about the doubt, as a tool to discriminate and ask yourself, "Is this what I really want to attract or not?" With your highly evolved power of discrimination--as long as you are not overshadowed by your emotions--you can tell what you want to attract and what you don't want to attract; what slows you down on your journey and what accelerates your bliss. Then, with the same power of pure discrimination, you can turn your attention to your feelings and they will help you identify and clarify your wanting. The density of the feeling makes itself known to you. You can almost see the particles of a feeling, sense their vibrations. Are they light or heavy? Are they fast or slow? Are they of the kind you want to attract or not? All this shouldn't take more than an instant, while you are on your non-stop journey.
Offer crystal clear discrimination. Cultivate it until, every moment of your life, it becomes second nature. Yes, no, yes, no, do it with ease. Not in order to exclude, but in order to progress, in grace and love. This is the meaning of life.

*I understand that the laws of the universe are the rules of the game of life. Can you explain these laws?*

Many people try to put into words the laws of the universe. They want stability. They want laws to tell them what they can and cannot do. Many of them have the right idea to some extent. But you do understand, that once you put laws into writing, it confines you, while We have already moved on in our journey. You see, even the word 'attraction' is somewhat limited. When you think of attraction, you think of something you desire, you get it, and that's the end. This is why I would rather call it the Law of change. It's attracting and maintaining balance on the go. This is the true meaning of 'live in the now.' This now is a split second, because a split second later you have a new thought which attracts a new creation. If your thought lingers on something you left behind, that is what you create again. Therefore, the only law is the Law of eternal moving, of ever-changing.

Everything moves, and what determines this movement is what you, the conscious human being, intend to do, intend to be. If you want to become a rich man, your game is different than someone who wants to become a monk, a prime minister, a teacher, or someone who wants to become a race car driver. It might seem like a paradox, but still, the only permanent truth is that there is nothing permanent.

*What about the Law of oneness?*

You see, if you are a particle that's called love, any particle in the world that's called love is one with you, by the Law of attraction.

*And 'as above so below' is the Law of oneness, too?*

This is you, expressing, out on the rim of the funnel, the blueprint of who you really are which comes from the Source. People call it above and below, I call it in and out. It is an eternal flow of in and out, in and out. The purer your reflection of who you are is, the purer your intentions are, the purer your thoughts and desires are-- the smoother the flow, the broader the understanding, the more magnificent your experience and creation.

*Experience of what? Of oneness and no separation?*

Yes. Experience of the blissful journey toward peace, harmony, truth; which is who you are. Because this is what you attracted to yourself. When you are in discord with the meaning of these words, when they are just words for you and not an experience, you know that your manifestation does not reflect who you really are. If you don't feel one with all of this and you offer discord, you are not in tune, as some people say. This is your measure of how you play this game, how in tune you are with the Law, because the Law is one. What do you do about it and how do you come back? By offering a pure desire from your heart you can leap forward. Desire and its manifestation are two sides of the same coin. They are already together, just a matter of flipping the coin. Being in the flow provides you with the excitement, exhilaration of the moving forward, of attracting the other side of the coin.

August 26, 1996

9

# 3

## Who Are You, God?

*I would like to ask a question which has been asked many, many times. Before we proceed I thought it would be proper to hear the answer from You. I'm asking it most humbly. Who are You? Can you help us to taste, to grasp, to understand, who You are?*

I am the totality of all there is. As your prophet put it into words in your holy book, I AM THAT I AM. Therefore, anything that anyone says, thinks, or experiences regarding who I Am, is only partial, unless merged with Me.

Merging with Me means being in the Source.

But those words, being and Source, are limited, because that is the nature of words.

Who I Am is unexplainable.

It's undefinable, since definition by its nature is bounded.

Words, by their nature, are bounded.

Nevertheless, I am calling you: come to Me.

I am announcing: I Am here and now.

I am telling you: Love Me as I love you.

By accepting Me as I Am, undefinable, unexplainable, you are taking your first step toward merging with Me.

Be the best you can, according to your awareness of Who I Am.

If you choose to follow the understandings or misunderstandings of your intellect, you live but a very partial life.

If you choose to say, "I don't understand, therefore I don't follow," and consider yourself very rational, you miss the opportunity to understand.

Don't look for definitions.

Open yourself to your potentiality, which is much more than your intellectual understanding.

The best expression the English language has for it is 'I Am.'

Be, and by being you come to understand Who I Am.
Don't ask Me, "Who are You?" Ask yourself, "Who am I?"
If there is something you do want to understand, it is who you are.
By being who you are, you come closer to understanding Who I Am.

*Is it correct to say that everything is Your kingdom, and all is God?*

Correct. God Is.

*Since we are always in Your kingdom, where does the merging with You come into play?*

Very well asked. The merging with Me implies oneness, implies the simple ability to create and uncreate yourself into the particles that make up all. To merge with Me means to be and not to be, at the same time. To be the seed and the tree, the thought and its manifestation, to be the ocean and the waves, to be the stillness and the motion, to be multidimensional, to be in the future, in the past, and focused in the present. You stretch your understanding of God being everywhere and in everything, and put it into the words omnipresent, omnipotent and omniscient, but these are still just verbal expressions. God Is. Keep the awareness of I Am.

Yes, it's all My kingdom, the beggar and the wealthy, the criminal and the righteous, peace and war, darkness and light. But did I create each one of these? No. I gave them the life force, I breathed life into them, as your Bible says. I gave them the very essence of Me, and the freedom to become who they are, creators. That freedom is expressed in creation, with all its beauties, multiple diversities, infinite possibilities. By choice, each one can return, collapse into the state of pure being. This is the ever-changing life that we talked about before. Even the highest, most massive, most magnificent mountains are changing all the time. And in this change there is the seed, the promise of perfection. Everything is on the move toward perfection, balance, and harmony.

11

So, coming back to your previous question, "Who is God?", never mind. God is just a name people made up. Who am I? I am a vast, infinite I that Is.

Now, probably nothing of this explanation really makes any sense. Therefore my request to you is, don't go only by your understanding. Be humble enough to accept who you are. Be humble enough to love who you are, because by accepting and loving who you are, you accept and love Who I Am.

*I am trying to feel where I fit in this vast, huge kingdom. Is it fair for the individual to say I am God?.*

It's more than fair, it is the truth. The little particle of sand on the shore is God, too. You are intelligent human beings. If you accept that God is everywhere and everything, why can't you accept that you are God?

*I hear people say: "Yes, I may be part of God, but I can't say I am God, I still feel like only one citizen of a huge kingdom."*

You are also that. You say God is everything. You are part of God and you are God. The problem lies in the fact that you assign value to everything. You judge everything as less or more, low or high, bad or good.

*Are you saying that the drop in the ocean is the ocean?*

The wisdom that's manifest in one atom of a fly, is the same wisdom that manifests in the most ingenious brain found in a human being. The drop in the ocean has all the elements of the ocean. The same creative intelligence that is in one atom, makes up the world.

*Is there good creation and bad creation?*

There is one that wants to merge with Me, and there is one that wants to part from Me.

*Is it possible to be in the Flow and still make war and bring hatred?*

You cannot be in the Flow while creating hatred. You can create your own momentum outside the Flow, which leads you nowhere and eventually falls apart.

*Is the reverse also true? If one increases love, light and justice, is he in the Flow and does he come closer to merging with You?*

You can say so. Because by the Law of attraction, this will bring more of its kind, and this is a never-ending expansion. Love is unconditional, infinite, while evil invites its own destruction. It cannot last.

*It is said that the Fall in the Garden of Eden was planned, and once we all merge with You, another scene will happen to create the drama again, to be an ongoing cycle. Is this so? Is there an end to this drama once all of us merge with You and live happily ever after?*

Creation is your free choice. What you do with it is your free choice. You were given the opportunity to create your world as you know it. You were given the building blocks. Everything that was needed was supplied, including your souls and your bodies. You chose to take it where you took it, and since it's an ongoing process, always changing, you could say that the drama will return and return and return. Even when you come back to the Source, the desire to manifest and create appears again and again. However, the drama will ever be different. Nothing happens in exactly the same way. There is always progress. There is always change.

Now, what is your purpose? Your purpose is to join the Flow, be ever on the move, ready to change, open to new possibilities.

Examine what prevents you from ever being on the move. Is it a judgment? Don't judge. Is it an attachment? Let go. Whatever holds you back, keeps you stagnant, miserable--get away from it. Don't hold on to it, because this is not who you are. What is it that holds you back? What is it that encourages you to hold on to hatred, pain, misery? It is despair, the feeling "there is nothing else for me," the feeling of emptiness, of "no one cares anyway." Therefore the message--God is here and now--turns on the light for you and says:

Wake up, clear away the dust. You are loved. You can get out and move on. There is no need to cling to your limitations any more. Uproot everything that originates from fear. God is everything, infinite possibilities. Join the team. By joining, separately and together, each one of you will be able to create new foundations for this world. By joining in the Flow, trusting in the Love, in the Light, and in the Life that move you forward, you create a revolution. But as long as you hold on to the mistaken understanding of being something other than God, you'll continue playing this game of inferiority. Rise above it. Become the God that you are.

August 27, 1996

4

## The Process of Creation

My dear children, like the current in the ocean that forms deep inside and carries its vibrations to the shore, so the peak of your life manifests as the waves meet the shore. Then, the waves fold back into the ocean, carrying with them what they met at the moment of contact, merging with the current as it progresses back to the Source. Your life at the peak of action, which occurs every moment, determines the content and quality of what will be carried back to the Source. The purer the content, the finer the content, the lighter the content, the more of it will come back to the Source.

At that moment of contact, when the stream of consciousness reaches the shore of action, you are omnipresent. You are fully there, determining the quality, like a grand designer. You have the power of the stream, tremendous power of consciousness. How do you put this power to use? By embracing the shore with love, whether it is rocky or sandy, lonely or crowded, beautiful or deserted. Bring to the shore the stream of consciousness, and with excitement and love, kiss it with your waters, wash it, and then come back, carrying with you everything you washed away--the sorrows and the happiness.

This is the nature of life, eternal and momentary at the same time. The stream will ever flow to the shore, but each wave is different from the previous one. Each wave has its own contact with the shore. In this contact the stream is fully there, free to experience the moment, and this experience determines its way back to the Source. This moment is constantly provided for you with much love, as if by a loving, patient father who plays with his child, adores him for every little movement, giggle, achievement. He gently teaches him, providing the opportunities and the toys, for more joy and progress. This is the life you came to experience. Just look around for the opportunities and the toys you can use to fully experience every moment with joy. Every moment is full of excitement. Only from excitement that springs from absolute security and love, can you fashion the content to create bliss.

*I would like to better understand the process of creation.*

From Nothingness, pure consciousness, no matter at all, no-form, creation unfolds. In this no-form, in this condensed Nothingness, there is power, tremendous power. All possibilities. This power has a desire to express itself, to come out of Nothingness, to experience its own power. This first desire, first impulse, to come out of all potentiality into a separate manifestation, sets into motion pure energy. You can call the first manifestation of something out of nothing, energy. So we are talking about an impulse, pure energy, and then creation.

Now let's understand this impulse. It is a pure thought. It is so pure that your mind cannot grasp its meaning. This pure thought is all love, is all good, and nothing other than that exists. In this seed of pure thought that is love and good, all of creation already exists. You call it 'blueprint.' This pure thought sets into motion pure energy that unfolds into creation. So, in essence, everything that is manifested was already in that thought, everything was latent in the power of Nothingness. When thought sets pure energy into motion, the first manifestation is Light. The pure energy manifests itself as primordial Light and primordial Sound, which are different frequencies of the energy that bursts forth to create. If a human being can attune himself to absolute silence, he can see the Light and hear the Sound.

Now, the energy is sent to the four corners of the universe. Pure thoughts and desires manifest into forms; energy changes into matter. The high vibration energy of primordial Light becomes denser and denser, slower and slower, and creates the different bodies of the universe.

At the primordial stage everything is still formless, as you perceive form with your senses. At this stage your light body was formed, which is a slightly lower vibration of energy. In the last stage of this process, the energy at its highest density creates your physical body-- matter as you know it, in the three dimensional world in which you live. There is life, existence and awareness in each one of the stages. Each atom, each particle of this universe exists in all stages all the time. This is the hardest part for you to comprehend, because you cannot see this truth or feel it with your senses. After all, your senses are tools for you to deal with this higher density only. In order for you to experience your reality in the less dense worlds, you need to develop a different set of tools. When I say develop, I actually mean re-member, because now that you've come all the way to the physical world, you need to go back and reconnect with what you knew before.

Most beings choose to go all the way to the physical world because the challenge is greater, the trip is longer, the contrast is clearer. What would you rather do, take a trip to the town square, or travel to Japan? Where would you see more, have more chances to deal with the contrast, learn new things about the environment and yourself?

You are potentially always in all of the worlds, but at different cycles you choose to focus on only one of them and function from there. Or you can go back to the Source altogether and rest for a while. This process never ends, because the Nothingness always wants to express and experience itself again and again and recreate. Does this make it clearer?

*Yes, thank you. I'd like to ask more specifically about the process of creation and re-creation in the physical world. Do I understand correctly that there are generally two ways to create? If I want a chair, I build it. The other way is through attracting it into my experience; I want a chair, I think about it, imagine myself having it and using it joyfully. Then I come upon my ideal chair at an affordable price at a garage sale, via the power of my thoughts and feelings. Can you explain this process of creation?*

Remember, everything already exists at some level as energy and your thoughts can direct this energy. So you can say, the energy is the chair and the thoughts direct the energy. Therefore what matters is how and where you direct your thoughts.

If your thought is, "The only way for me to have a chair is by building it," that is how it will be manifested for you. If your thought is, "The only way for me to have a chair is by buying it," you will see it in a catalog or a garage sale or in a store or somebody will knock at your door and sell it to you. If you believe in the possibility that the only way to have a chair is by manifesting it directly from thin air, you will be able to do it without any problem. It is as simple as that, because the chair already exists in some stage of condensation of energy. If you can offer a really focused, pure thought of the exact details of the chair, it will be condensed in front of your eyes from what you call 'thin air.' There is really no such thing as thin air. It's all moving vibrations that were created by thoughts. You can either call everything matter, or call nothing matter. See the point? Did I answer your question?

*Yes. Thank you. Can you talk about integrating thoughts, intentions and inner guidance with intellectual decision making?*

The discriminative mind is essential but it is not enough. You need to use your intuition as a bridge to lead you from the intellectual knowing to your higher knowing. What helps you to follow your intuition? Your feelings. They are your intuition's best friends. Always follow your intuition. Let the intellect, the mind, be your servant. The mind is your tool, but not the one that leads the way.

The beauty of your intuition is that it comes effortlessly, whenever you need it. Train yourself to follow it. This is the gathering of your energies into one point in order to bring about manifestation. Your ultimate goal is to be able to do that with one instant of pure focused intention.

Remember that whatever you do, you want it to be the product of your whole Being, not only of your intellect. That means that you need to trust the process of going within. Most of all, you need to trust, just as you trust that the sun will rise in the morning, that you will manifest your desired creation.

*In our lives we want to manifest many things at the same time. How does that work?*

It is very important for you to focus on one thing at a time, because only then can you manifest it in the shortest possible time. You focus on many things throughout your day from moment to moment. You can play with this focus, putting some in the background and some in the foreground. The more energy you flow toward one focus the more powerful it will be. Therefore, it helps to have only one focus at a time in the foreground. Funneling of energy is needed but don't let it go too soon, or the cycle won't be completed. The energy will be scattered before it manifests. When you have completed the stage that summons the energy, you can trust that the energy will continue working for you. Then you can turn your attention to a different goal. You need to focus for a while and then let go, having trust all the way. This is how you create.

You must train yourself to be one-pointed so all your energies will actually penetrate the delicate passageway to infinity. Your power of creation depends on your willingness to focus and be the navigator. Then you will find that, in no time you move forward at a speed you never imagined possible. Your wheels are already moving but this one-pointedness will be like stepping on the gas. Think boldly of what you want and focus on it, in thoughts and actions. You'll be the starter and I'll be the car. Together we'll climb the mountains.

*On a different note, what made God decide to create the human soul?*

This is a primordial question that takes you back to a very profound aspect of your existence. The human soul is an outcome of God's desire to express Itself, of God's desire to give, of God's desire to love. Consciousness desires and sets into motion energy that creates matter. Therefore matter can be understood only in its connection to the Source.

The human soul originates from a very deep desire in the Heart of God, which functions from love. This Heart desires expression and wants to experience Itself through Its counterpart that reflects the Heart. Out of this Heart that desired came creation, which received shape and form and life of its own. The human soul is part of this creation and was created as an expression of God's desire to experience Itself. The human soul is there to enable a relationship between the Heart and the human Heart, a relationship of never-ending giving and receiving; a relationship of Love between the Creator and His creation. This Love is the essence. The human soul reflects the qualities of this Heart; therefore, it cannot be separated from It.

When God decided to create the human soul, it was not an act of separation, of creating and letting go. It was the creation of a reflection. The reflection cannot exist without its source--they are one. A human soul is a reflection of God--they are one. The Creator and His creation are one.

April 19, 1996
August 28, 1996

## 5

## Milestones on the Way to God Realization

By striving to understand Me, you open the pathways for the Light to shine through, to create broader comprehension. Your inquiry initiates the process of expansion of awareness. This expansion happens when the Light is turned on simultaneously on all levels of your being, while you stay open, truly desiring to be in the flow of change, recreating yourself, rearranging yourself. The inquiry can originate in different places, depending on the individual. In a mind-oriented individual, most likely the inquiry will come through the intellect. But the effect of the desire that originates from the heart is not less; it may be even more powerful. Truly there is no difference; it is just a different flavor of the same desire to know Me. With a strong intellect and a pure heart the expansion of awareness happens.

Some individuals become too emotional, sometimes losing the path, forgetting what they truly desire. Others become too intellectual, losing themselves in the details, focusing on the parts, sometimes even idolizing the parts, believing in them to bring results or salvation. Good communication between mind and heart indicates both balance between them, and a certain degree of mastery over them. This balance manifests in a healthy environment of the different bodies--physical, emotional and mental. It eases progress and keeps it whole.

Your awareness of your different bodies and their different functions in your being enables you to see the grander vision of your wholeness. But when the tendency of the being is to put attention on only one of the bodies, disharmony is created, which slows down the process of joining the flow toward infinity. By nature, you strive to be balanced because from balance within, you can develop a greater vision of who you are. Balance is the foundation from which you can feel excitement, express pure thoughts and manifest your desires. From deep rest and stillness within, a place of balance, peace and harmony, you come forth with desires and excitement to create.

How do you reach balance, harmony and peace? Drop anything that indicates non-balance, such as stress, wrong diets, too much sex--whatever translates in your understanding as non-balance. Then create balance and harmony for yourself because nobody can do it for you. Nobody can bring another human being into peace and balance. I would say this is probably the greatest mission for mankind at this time and place--to come back to the balance from which you can recreate everything that was miscreated.

And how do you create? For this you were given your absolutely brilliant discriminative mind and your feelings. Together they are your tools, helping you to discover what you want to create, and initiate a process to discover who you are. But remember, these are faculties that were given you to handle all that comes to you from the outside.

You are like a butterfly going from flower to flower, exploring and tasting a little bit here, a little bit there, for the purpose of existing, of being, of multiplying, of flowing, of blissfully flying in the sun. Like the butterfly, you can flow with your whole being, using outer and inner faculties. What are your inner faculties and how do you access them? For this you were given your intuition. The more you refine your mind and your feelings, the more your intuition grows. Your intuition connects your five senses with your inner world. Your intuition is the bridge between doing and being, activity and stillness. And if you develop your intuition even further you can reach a state of free flow, absolute connection, where you feel you are guided. You feel that something else moves you, rather than your external wanting. Then you are in the Flow and you experience oneness. You trust the process and whatever you need is supplied.

The whole range of tools is available to you. But to begin with, you need to accept and believe that there is more to everything than you now perceive. You need to declare, and bring into awareness that God is here and now. Open the door so all those possibilities and experiences will find a way to come to you. Open the door, because there is nothing to lose, nothing to fear.

*Can you please speak about the relationship between being and doing in our lives?*

In a state of being there is a subtle moving forward, striving to be one with God. It is a process, though not a very visible one. It is not on the level of doing anything as an active physical doing. It is funneling energy. You live in the world of doing, a world of big and small obligations, a world of everyday life. This world seems far away from what you call 'the spiritual realm' and I call 'the inner world.' They seem to you to be parallel, as if one can be spiritual at certain times but needs to be practical at other times. People say, "Well, this is nice, but I have to be practical," or, "This was a nice book," but they keep on doing what they always do. There is no integration of what is spiritual and what is daily life, of what is doing and what is being. How can you combine these two? How can you realize and understand that there are no two? How can you see the inner world in the outer world? How can you see that being and doing are one?

I Am One. I Am everywhere. I Am everyone. I Am everything there is. I Am the doing and the being. I Am the relative and the absolute. I Am the outer and the inner. I Am the layers and the wholeness. I Am One. What can be more obvious than that? Why can't you just accept it and live it? You can not live it because your mind is in your way again, saying, "I say two, I sense four, I hear five, I see the details. How can it all be one?" Your mind does not support what your heart tells you. Your mind is deceived by what seems to you to be true, because you don't listen to your heart.

Stop for a moment. Stop everything. Close your eyes. Stop your thoughts. Stop the noise. Stop the nitty-gritty of your mind. What do you hear? Nothing. One vast Nothingness. Can you feel it? When you stop, you feel the Nothingness that envelopes you. It penetrates you and goes through everything. It is everywhere. Everywhere is pervaded by this Nothingness. It spreads like fog. It becomes everything. This is Me. This is Me being One. This is Me being everything. There is no separation. I Am that Nothingness that penetrates everything. There is no separation between the no-thing and the thing. The only difference is 'no.' It is all One. Can you feel it?

Open your eyes. Now you can let it all come in again. You hear the train in the distance, the children playing outside, the clock ticking next to you. It's all spilling in again--your thoughts, everything around you, all come in again. Does it take away the Nothingness? No. They coexist. There is room for everything. There is no separation. You can be doing and being at the same time. You can have thoughts and stillness at the same time. You can have noise and silence at the same time. You can have a busy schedule and deep rest at the same time. They coexist. There never was a separation. It is you who gave them different names. It's all One.

When you have this oneness in your heart, it fills your heart. It fills you, thrills you. There is room for everything in your heart. Your heart is as big as the ocean, as big as the universe, as big as Me, because I Am your heart. You are I and I Am you. In this heart there is no separation, there is no excluding, no hatred, no 'excepts'-- it contains all. Can you feel it in your heart? This is Love. No one can take it away from you. It is the most wonderful feeling you can have. When you love, you are one, one with yourself and everything around you. It's like glue, it connects you all.

Now, how can you contain this Love in your heart when the mind keeps on saying, "Not this, not that, this is ugly, that's disturbing, that's different, that's not like me?" Oh, how good and lovely it would be if your mind and heart could work together. Let your mind observe, but let your heart decide. Let the mind examine, but let the heart be the final judge. Let the mind collect the data, but let the heart fill in the blanks to create a whole. Open the gates of your heart to create oneness.

What do you do? You feed your heart with the information from the mind, but forget to feed the mind with the information from the heart. When you keep both pathways open, nothing will be overwhelming. The mind will be balanced by the heart and the heart will be balanced by the mind. You'll flow naturally in this oneness, enjoying this oneness. The doing and the being will coexist. No separation. All things will be imbued with beingness, with Nothingness. They won't stand there by themselves calling, "Look at me, look at me, pay attention!" They will be part of a whole, in balance. Your life will be what life should be--joy, no struggle. Your life will be like a stream flowing downward, joyfully flowing over little rocks and big rocks. Kissing both banks of the river, touching the trees, rising with the wind, feeding the fish, happily flowing. Bubbles of water, rising and falling, sometimes lively, sometimes quiet, sometimes in a narrow stream, sometimes in a wide open valley. Always flowing easily, with joy, to the ocean. This is life.

*You said: I Am you. What do You mean by that?*

I Am you is the essence of everything I teach. I Am you is oneness. I Am you is unity. Note, I don't say, "I and you or I plus you," but rather, "I Am you." I Am you says in three simple words that I Am everywhere, I Am everybody, I Am also in you. There is no separation between you and Me. I Am in the gaps. I Am in the essence. I Am in the molecules. I Am in the air around you. I Am That I Am and you are that you are and both are One. Oneness is what I desire to bring to each and every heart. Oneness is what I desire people to experience, to understand and be. Oneness will bring peace and Heaven on Earth, because it will come from within you and flow naturally. It is inherent in you. It won't require effort or enforcement, it will come peacefully. Heaven on Earth is so close. All you have to do is to feel it, to be it. Let go of all the problems and complications you create for yourselves. Consciously let go of all doership. This letting go, consciously making the choice to *not do*, will lead you to effortless activity.

*Even though the journey is very personal can you describe common milestones on the way to God realization?*

The milestones are: accepting, believing and Understanding. The first milestone is the acceptance of God--recognizing that there is something that lies beyond the self. It is recognition of God's oneness. In accepting God's oneness there is a wide variation of experience. It could be expressed in the simple desire for more love, and in the deep yearning of the heart to belong. This first step of yearning usually leads the person on a journey to seek for more experience and evidence, so he can believe.

Believing is the next milestone--trusting that there is something that lies beyond the self. It is believing in God's oneness--not necessarily calling it God. When people are established in believing, their journey takes on a devotional shift to a path, a sage, a tradition, a religion, thrusting the journey onto some higher wisdom.

The final milestone is Understanding--knowing the oneness of God. Knowing God's oneness equals God realization. It is not an intellectual understanding but the whole being's understanding of oneness. The being realizes that everything which preceded was just a journey, an attempt to reach from one place to another, while all along the being was already present, here and now.

August 29, 1996
October 16, 1995

# 6

## Real Mastery in Every Moment

Today's message is threefold. You've received the explanation of how the funnel works, how your innermost faculties cooperate with your outer faculties to create wholeness. This wholeness always exists in the background. You have the ability to focus on each part separately in different cycles and activities at the foreground. And you can also bring the parts to wholeness as you let wholeness be established in the foreground.

Your focus can change in three cycles: in different dimensions, in different intentions, and from moment to moment. The more expanded and inclusive the cycle is, the closer you are to the Source. When the decision was made to incarnate in your physical embodiment in this dimension, you were given the tools to focus and operate mainly in this dimension. Here is your challenge: to remember that your existence in the physical world is just an outer extension, that in addition you have many inner faculties, and that you are at all times connected to wholeness, to the Source. Therefore you can function simultaneously as a whole and in one focal point. Real mastery means using all tools in any dimension, any time. And by choice, by will power, operate them as needed in different stages on the long funnel from the innermost to the outermost worlds.

When you are at the Source stage, still in the form of a thought, you are all potentiality. But once you choose a specific mission, the tendency is to forget the wholeness and to remain in the focus. This is true for all dimensions, not only the physical, even though in the physical dimension, the forgetting is probably the most intense. Therefore, to choose this dimension, this focus, is the highest challenge for a soul to experience. The greatest mastery that one can achieve is to be able to travel at will between all the possibilities. For this, you need to open your channels, to allow the energy from the innermost worlds to reach the outermost; to allow the consciousness, the wisdom that sent you on this mission in the first place, to pour through, so to speak, so that you can get instructions from your 'headquarters' about what to do in your present 'station.'

Most become so focused on their physical environment that they believe this is the only reality that exists. Their physicality overshadows everything else. But in reality, it is not a matter of which aspect of your existence comes first and which comes next, of what's more important and what's less important--it's a matter of wholeness and parts co-existing. What would you rather hear, a part of the symphony or the whole symphony? You should be able to choose to hear any part you want, but to fully enjoy it, you want to hear the whole thing. Same with your life.

Now I would like to go farther, to the level of intentions, and assume that you have the desire to experience the wholeness and its parts simultaneously. How do you go about it? First must come total acceptance of this knowingness, total absorption. You need to be absorbed in the reality of wholeness as a way of life, not just as an intellectual concept. Always have the awareness of wholeness within yourself. Trust that you are in the right place at the right time, and at every moment attune yourself to your power, to the stream that connects you to all. From this basis you can develop the ability to visit any station on the way to the Source. Your soul can travel consciously between the dimensions. With this understanding, the meaning of death changes. You can focus your intention in different dimensions in infinite ways. I tell you here and now that this is a reality. By nature you have the ability to focus at any time on anything you wish, and become that.

Now let's see how you can express this ability from moment to moment. When you are born, your life is given to you like a big chunk of nice wet clay. You are the one who gets to shape it and reshape it. The big question is: Who is the 'you?' Since most people are lost in their physicality and believe this is the only focus that exists, they think that the 'you' includes only the physical, mental and emotional bodies. But you already know that the 'you' is much broader than that. This broader 'you' is involved in the play of shaping the clay. One may ask, is there a divine plan or free will in this shaping? Confusion arises from the lack of understanding that 'who you are' can be at any point on a long continuum between God and man. 'Who you are' encompasses the entire continuum. Therefore, both divine plan and free will operate.

You are able to flow in the never-ending process of growth to the extent that you allow your inner self to be expressed in decision making. If you have the notion that a decision regarding one incarnation or another is tremendously important, while a decision about your daily life is less important, you are mistaken. A moment in your life is also a moment in infinity; there is no difference. Every moment is divinity. At every moment you can choose to be any of the parts or bring wholeness to the parts. Let's take the example of Dorit's tiredness today. She can choose to be her body and say, "Oh, I am tired and I cannot do anything." Or she can say, "Yes, my body is tired, but the rest of me is alert, I can do anything."

Infinite possibilities exist at every moment. How does this apply to your life? By using your discriminative mind and your feelings at every moment, keeping the balance of the heart and the mind, you can choose to smile or to frown, to be loving or to be hateful. By using the tools you have been given, including your higher understanding and your trust in the wholeness, you can choose to be angry or to be kind, to be generous or to be greedy, to appreciate or to criticize. This is called Conscious Living. Remember, you are here because some conscious force created you, and since you were created out of consciousness, you are consciousness.

Your discriminative mind along with your personal talents, personal lessons and desires, can be used, moment to moment, to bring into full expression different aspects of your being. This is the interplay of life. This is the beauty of life. You are all parts in a big wholeness, and what you do adds to the wholeness. If you want the symphony to be beautiful, add only beautiful notes to it. If you don't pay attention or don't care, you add discord to it and then are surprised that the symphony doesn't sound so good.

So now I believe we have created a broader perspective to understand what it is all about. We have laid a foundation in which everyone can find himself or herself, and ask, "Where am I in this funnel? What else do I need to do to be in touch with wholeness?" And now we can deal with other topics. Is this all right with you?

August 30, 1996

## 7

## Reorientation in Education

We've laid the foundation for the understanding of Who I Am, who you are , and what the relationship between Us is. We've laid the foundation for the understanding of the game of life, the main principles of how it works and how everyone can find himself in relation to the game. The general outline is drawn. Numerous things could still be said, but the man or woman with an open heart and mind, by now has the necessary tools to find the answer to almost any question they might have, based on the foundation we have laid.

Nevertheless as I promised, we will deal with separate topics, since the curious mind wants answers, wants to see the relevance of the 'philosophical' understanding to everyday life, which now is still only a theory for most. The theory has to be chewed and chewed until there is a willingness to turn it into an experience. I want to make it relevant, to touch on new topics, and show how the parts are connected to the whole. But I want you to step forward, after you have arranged everything logically in your mind, and dive into the unknown, take the 'risk' and give Me a chance. What would you like to begin with?

*The first topic I would like to ask about is education. Who is the ideal teacher? What is the ideal relationship of teacher and student, and what is the highest knowledge we need to learn and teach?*

Very well. Education implies that someone has the responsibility to influence or teach others. It's true that one can educate oneself, but mostly education is conceived of as a relationship between teacher and student in different settings which involve class, school, and the education system as a whole. While this understanding of education arose from the need to share knowledge with 'less educated' people, it turned into a very conceptualized assumption that one or a few knew more than others. Since they felt they knew more, they took upon themselves the presumptuous responsibility of giving knowledge to those who knew less, often without asking them whether they wanted or needed it.

Education can be done in infinite ways, forums and relationships. The most common ways are in schools, with adults and children, and to some degree, in the family. The reason that I say to some degree is that most families today assume that education is given in school, so they leave this to the teachers. Thus we have a group of people assuming responsibility to share their knowledge, and sometimes even force it on another group of people, the children.

Now let's examine this assumption. On what basis does society decide that the teachers' training is preparing them to help children learn? Furthermore, why do educators assume that what they were taught is what the child needs in order to grow?

Well, everything seems to be right in place, so why doesn't it work? Why is it that millions of children go to school and in many cases don't like it and find it boring? Why is it that you need so many years to teach basic math, reading skills and a few history facts that could be acquired in a shorter time? The reason is that the fundamental assumption at the base of this massive organization is faulty, is a mistake.

When a child is born--no matter which child, no matter what qualities he was given at birth--whether he's healthy or sick, able or disabled as you call it, he is a whole unit. This unit is designed for the sole purpose of learning, developing, progressing, growing, experiencing every bit of experience that the life span he is planning to spend here is going to give him. When you buy a computer you assume that it will 'know' all the things you need it to do for you. It comes packaged. You just feed the computer your ideas and the computer produces what you need. Many adults regard the child the same way, like a computer that is fed with the correct information in order to produce results. But while the computer is passive and is fed only what you feed it, the child has his own consciousness, his own inclinations, his own desires, his own specific reasons for exploring life. The child is a completely unique unit and because of this uniqueness there is not one system, not one answer that suits all.

Children have the capacity to observe their surroundings. Their means of observation are quite different from an adult's, who often considers himself a 'finished product,' who already knows everything and has acquired the necessary education to become a man or woman, functioning in society. The way a child absorbs knowledge is by using all his faculties, not only logic. A child has the ability to read between the lines, to hear between the words, to sense what's in the heart, to feel the nuances of the ever-changing happenings that he is witnessing on his 'outer screen.' At the same time the child has the innate ability to draw from his own inner being, to digest what he has seen, heard, sensed and felt, and to imprint it on his 'inner screen.' By accumulating impressions, he builds an identity and creates within himself the connection between the outer and the inner.

A child comes with a complete, clear, pure, inner world and has the potential to develop and grow in any given direction. From the moment he opens his eyes he is busy collecting impressions from the outer screen and matching them with the inner, building a new identity, a new creation.

Now you can understand how important it is what the child sees, what the child feels, what the child absorbs. Does the scenery on the outer screen that he is witnessing match the scenery on the inner screen? Is it in harmony with his inner picture or does it offer discord? A child opens his eyes into a smiling loving face, absorbs what he sees, feels, hears, and senses. The match is done instantaneously. A little layer of confidence is built. The new creation begins on a good foundation. Now, if the child sees an angry face, and hears a screaming voice, feels an unpleasant touch, he absorbs this, and it does not match his inner pure being. A discord is offered, a crack is formed in the foundation. This happens many times during the days and years of the child's growth.

The more the outer world matches the inner world, the stronger, the more beautiful and more glorious the child's being grows. Moreover, the stronger this foundation is, the more the child's ability to absorb knowledge grows, exponentially. When the outer screen offers seeds to match the child's interests, spontaneously he desires to learn; spontaneously he develops interests according to his inclination in life. So even if the child never went to school, the ever-changing movement on the screen of his life would teach him numerous things.

Look at your children. Don't they learn to crawl, walk, speak, eat, use tools and play in a very brief time, all before they go to school? It is when outer impressions try to control and erase parts on the inner screen--this is yes, this is no, this you should, and this you shouldn't--that the pure system of reflection and absorption begins to be confused. Instead of the child absorbing as much as he is able and needs to at a given moment, he is told that he must learn at these hours, these subjects, by these teachers under these conditions. He is told that if he doesn't, he will face some unpleasant consequences. If he does, he will be rewarded. Positive reinforcements or negative reinforcements are still reinforcements. They are still an attempt to direct from outside an internal world that knows spontaneously and intelligently what to do.

Now you wonder what this implies. Does it imply the cancellation of the education system as you know it? For the most part, yes. The present education system has to go through a revolutionary change. The basic assumptions have to change. The new basic assumption must be that a child learns spontaneously and when he comes to school the excitement will be maintained for as long as learning continues and won't be suppressed by a system, by a teacher, or by a schedule. When the child feels complete in his absorption for that day he will be allowed to leave or do something else exciting, but won't be made to wait patiently, bored, for the 'projection on the screen' to change.

In other words, school has to be a place that offers a field of all possibilities, where a child can find points of interest to invigorate his innate curiosity. Yes, this place should be supervised by very knowledgeable adults who are there at the right time, to answer the child's questions. Sounds messy? Mess is just a frame of mind, coming from the assumption that there should be a certain kind of order. But order is an innate quality in the universe, it is not necessarily the order you have in your mind. If you follow this innate quality, you cannot help but be in this order. If the child is used to learning this way from the day he comes into this world, he will naturally know how to use his freedom. Whether he completes a lesson in five minutes or in an hour or in ten hours, he will be totally following his innate order. The same is true in the family, the neighborhood school, high school, and college. The same is true of the educational assistance more developed countries give to developing countries.

This change might shake the education industry, and the careers of many people. Believe Me, it will save you a lot of money and a lot of time, because what the child now acquires in 12 years, can be done in a much shorter time.

The current educational system is based on the assumption that adults know and determine what children should learn. Now, one may ask: "What if half the children are not interested in a 'required' subject and all they are interested in is video games?" Probably it won't happen. What might happen is that by nature, the child will be inclined to one specific area. If he is exposed to all possibilities, he will try many, and learn them to some degree, in order to support the one area he is drawn to. If he is not interested in a given subject at a particular time, that is also very well.

It all has to do with the educators' trust in the child's innate ability to monitor his own progress. There is always room for encouragement; there is always room for introducing new subjects; but there is never room for reinforcement and control. There is only room for a loving relationship, for growth together and for shared adventure. In this kind of educational environment, values, respect, friendliness, acceptance of who you are and acceptance of what others are, will not be merely words or subjects to be learned, but will be practiced and experienced. The whole notion of comparison and competition will change. The desire for excellence will come from within, as inner desire for growth rather than as a desire to impress someone.

Learning is a process that comes from within. It is an innate ability. Just as you don't have to teach a child how to use his senses, you don't have to teach a child how to learn. You just need to be there for him as an example. You have to be there for him to provide the stimuli, open the window of possibilities, so he can choose, excel, and go beyond. Most important of all, you as an adult, an educator, have to *be* what you teach, since a child learns not only by seeing and hearing but by example. If your mouth says one thing and your heart expresses something else, the child is confused and learns not to trust you and others, because what he gets doesn't match his inner world, which is all innocence. You are like an open book when you approach a child. Only if you are willing to remain open can you work with children. Otherwise you damage more than you help.

*What kind of guidance does a teacher need to provide to a student?*

The guidance has to come from a feeling of humility, of sharing rather than telling. It has to come from an attitude that says, "This is what I have accumulated so far. Do you want me to share it with you?"

*How does ideal education apply to specific training, for example, to become a physician?*

A person's desire to help and heal others is a deep, innate desire. It comes solely from within, not because of social standards or monetary rewards. A physician who is a healer with all his mind, heart and soul, can trace his desire to heal back to his childhood. As a child he was naturally inclined to absorb information and to look at situations that needed healing. As a student who wants to be a professional healer, he looks for appropriate schooling to help him. And if so many years of preparation and learning are required, the student will gladly and relatively easily do it all, since it matches his own inner desire to heal.

*Do we already have an ideal educational system, such as home schooling or individual learning? Which one is closest to ideal education?*

There are many people who have awakened to this truth. You have schools around the world that are trying to apply education based on the assumption that the child learns spontaneously.

*Like home schooling, for example?*

Home schooling in itself doesn't guarantee anything, but it is probably one of the most ideal units for education, if the adults involved understand the principles we have discussed. If the adults supply ever-fresh and nourishing scenery on the outer screen to reflect and match the inner screen, they will be a living example for the child. They need to provide the right feeling level for the child. They need to provide opportunities for the child to choose and learn what he is inclined to, for the purpose of growth--not an easy task in the present society.

*Would ideal education create a happier people and better professionals?*

Yes. students will have a more positive outlook on society and be more innocent as a whole. What's most important, they will be able to make the connection between their inner world and their outer world and will be able to grasp and understand the unity of everything. They will take responsibility for their own growth and their own definition of who they are. They will be more flexible when facing the fluctuations of life, and more whole as an individual unit. Students in ideal education won't experience those cracks in personality that you so often find in this modern world, because the students' outer picture will match beautifully their inner picture. They will be clear about who they are in all aspects of life.

*Will they be greater inventors and more creative scientists?*

Yes, if this is what their inclination is. In ideal education they won't be framed, fenced, stopped, monitored and made to think in terms of staged progress. Time won't be a limiting factor, the way it is in school today, where you break learning into a semester, a quarter, into 45 minute classes, as if you can box learning. Some individuals break out of this limiting factor. You hear about 'genius' children who go to college when they are 14 years old. They were just able to focus their innate abilities without being stopped.

*What will the positive influence be on future generations in business, politics, etc.? How will ideal education bear fruits in other fields of life?*

Respect for diversity, acceptance of differences, functioning with ease, producing for the good of all, functioning from love rather than fear, and trusting in the process.

*What about competition? Can you talk about how this will manifest? What is the value, if any, of competition?*

The only value of competition is in a context where everyone respects each other and accepts others as having equal rights to express and excel. In such an environment there is no need to control or show superiority. When each human being sees God in others, competition takes on an entirely different meaning. Competition becomes a way of expressing the joy of excellence. If one runs faster, or gets to the goal first, or produces more, everyone rejoices for the benefit of the whole. Since everyone is established in his own being, another's winning doesn't create a feeling of unworthiness or insecurity. It is a recognition of the other person's ability to excel in his own special unique way, while fully trusting that, "I will excel in my own special unique way." Then, competition is a beautiful opportunity to express joy, togetherness and appreciation.

*How about competition to stimulate students to make more demands on themselves, to focus more?*

Not recommended. It's a way of manipulating. You have to trust the student and his own innate curiosity to excel. There are numerous ways in which you can encourage excellence.

*Who is the ideal teacher?*

Me. Quite arrogant, huh? Life! However, if a person is blind to life he needs a teacher. I was not joking when I said Me. Being Me implies being and doing simultaneously. Be connected to your Source at all times, even in the midst of activity. A teacher who stands in a class and angrily screams: "I want you to be good!" draws only laughter from his students. A teacher who can be and do at the same time, who, by example, is being what he wants the students to become, is the best teacher.

If you have a desire to become a teacher, ask yourself, "What do I want to teach? Am I ready for the responsibility? Does it excite me, scare me, elate me?" Check how you feel about it. Then set aside all those questions, listen to your intuition, your inner guidance and you will know whether you are supposed to be a teacher or not. Not everyone is a teacher. You don't become a teacher for the salary. Any teaching is an important responsibility.

*So, does the first change need to come on the level of expanded awareness and broader understanding of the teachers?*

Of course, but not only the teachers. The teachers are only part of this huge system and the system needs to change.

*This change demands a great expansion of awareness. Is it realistic to expect such a dramatic change?*

That's why We are writing this book.

*The implications of changing the entire system are so far reaching, where can we even begin?*

The framework, the buildings, the hours can stay the same to begin with. But when the child enters the school, he will enter a different world, a world of all possibilities. The enthusiasm of the children will be so great that there will be virtually no misbehavior. The need for control will be absent. If you come to think of it, it's really not so complicated. It is just a reorientation.

*Maybe we need a new definition of the objective of education, the purpose of education. Not to prepare better professionals, but to prepare whole and joyful human beings?*

Absolutely right! This is part of the reorientation. For this to happen, the consciousness of all citizens has to shift from control to trust--trust in the child's innate ability to learn, trust in the unfolding of the learning process. Most of all, the consciousness has to shift to accepting, believing and Understanding that there is a higher order and a higher purpose in life. It all leads us back to God is here and now.

August 31, 1996

# 8

## Godliness in Relationships

Good morning. What a good and lovely morning it is. Let's all bathe in the warmth of the sun. Stop thinking for a minute. It is so nice just to be. Leave everything outside this room, all the yesterdays and all the tomorrows. Just be, and imagine that everyone and everything in his own unique way is just being.

I want to talk to you today about relationships, how to see God in everyone. When you come from a place of ease, of an inner smile, of a new beginning that started a second ago, it is so easy to smile at everyone. It is so easy to accept everyone and wonder at the perfection of the moment. Because in this new beginning there is no data about how it used to be or how it is supposed to be; it is being. It is there in front of your eyes, reflecting your own smile back to you. The next moment is just a surprise; sometimes a good surprise, sometimes not such a pleasant one. What do you do then? Do you go back to yesterday, to your set of values of how and what is supposed to be, or do you draw from your inner ease, your inner smile? This is exactly the challenge that you all face. It's very easy to admire nature when it's green and clean and shining. It's very easy to admire lovely healthy children playing. It's easy to be generous when you have a lot to share. It's easy to see God in a smiling face.

But is it easy to see God in yourself, to admire what's in yourself? Is it easy to release yourself from the need to catalogue everything, compare and judge all the ideas you have gathered and have been taught--what's beautiful, what's correct, what is spiritual, what is Godly and what is not? If you keep this set of well-defined, dichotomous concepts in your mind, you are always busy comparing and judging. This is almost an instinct of yours. You cannot avoid it unless you consciously drop it. Accept yourself as you are, and love what you see.

What if you don't like qualities you see in yourself? Accept them nevertheless as yours, because they are yours. Any attempt to justify them won't help. They are still yours. You are 'stuck with them!' The only way to clear these qualities out of your system is first to accept them. This is what they wanted in the first place. They wanted your attention. If you continue judging yourself, not liking what you see, and fighting it, that is what you'll continue seeing for the rest of your life. It will knock on your door for attention again and again, from inside and outside of you. Accept what you see. Say to yourself, "I recognize you, I don't like what you offer but I accept you as mine because I created you. Now I let you go." One by one you will let the qualities you don't like in yourself go. What will remain then is you, the smiling you that you knew existed all the time. That smiling you will again be at ease. Again it will be easy to love what you see, and when it is easy to love what you see in yourself, it's easy to love what you see in others.

If you have learned to accept your own anger, you can accept someone else's anger. If you have learned to accept your own limitations and let them go, you can accept someone else's limitations and let them go. If you have learned to see the smiling you, you can see the smile in everyone. The relationship between you and yourself is your barometer for your relationship between you and others. Drop your judgments, your expectations, your disappointments and your comparisons. If you want to change, focus on the change. If you want to be other than what you manifest--desire, state your goal and manifest it the way you want. Don't waste your time on mourning, "If only I had done this or that..." Every moment of your life is Life. It is not yesterday and it is not tomorrow that matters. It is the desire that you set *now* that matters. Be the visionary of yourself. If there is a reason why you don't like what you see, envision what you do want to be and know that who you are is even more magnificent than you can imagine.

If you stand firm in the belief that inside you there is a perfect smiling child, a child of God, how can you not see that child in another human being? It is when you doubt this perfection in yourself, that it is easy to doubt the perfection in others. From this place of ease and inner smile you can feel secure in your relationships with others. Then, even what seems less than perfect in them has nothing to do with your perfection. It has only to do with the limitations they have created for themselves.

There are probably numerous questions in your mind right now, such as: "What if I prefer one person over another? What if people are intruding into my wholeness? How do I convey my perfection to others? What if they don't think I am so perfect? What do I do if people are mean to me?" These are all valid questions, and they are all situations with which you often have to deal. When such situations seem overwhelming how can you bridge the gap between the apparent reality and your inner ease? Remember that if you keep wholeness in your background and focus on only one situation in the foreground at a time, this situation will be resolved and it will go back to the bank of wholeness, to give rise to another focus at the foreground. This cycle is predictable and works with ease, when you are established in wholeness. The same principle works in relationships.

Once you learn to accept and love who you are, and always meet that smiling child within, your wholeness will help you to bring into focus the best way to deal with any situation. Your wholeness will always be there to support you, and will be so effective that the problem will dissolve before your eyes. The raging person who stands before you will soon realize that there is nothing to push against, to fight, there is really no thing and no one to be angry at. The very person who is trying to intrude, overtake, control, or annoy will have to retreat because he will find his methods ineffective. Sooner or later he will leave your presence. He will either change or find his own kind, for more lessons, trials and errors, until he reaches the same conclusion. The people who will come to you instead will be attracted to the form of communication that you offer, because the wholeness you radiate will bring them into ease, which is the most natural state of being. Anything that is out of ease is out of balance.

Balance is where you want to be at the beginning point of every action and interaction. This is where you begin, and your beginnings occur at every moment, so at every moment you want to be in balance. You live with the belief that the beginning is only the first day of the year, the first day of the month, the first day of school, first day of work--many firsts. But a beginning occurs every moment of your life. Every moment you have a chance to start with a clean slate. This is the basis for relationships.

*What about intimate relationships? Can you speak about finding a mate?*

Many of you wonder about this. You travel from one end of the world to another to find your mate. You consult with astrologers, psychologists and psychic people in your search for the one who will be the fulfillment of your dreams. But any attempt of yours to control the process, usually attracts the wrong mate. It's only when you relax that you meet the right one, in a most unexpected way, because it couldn't have happened any other way. What makes this meeting different, more special than any other meeting? A memory is evoked that quickens the heartbeat, when you meet that special one that you were dreaming of, the one who is none other than You in a different body. Since you have learned to love yourself you meet yourself again. In that moment of 'falling in love,' you are one soul, one being. What makes you one is the knowing that this is the only place where you want to be, completely being in the moment. You forget everything and everyone else.

'Falling in love' happens when your eyes meet and the memory is rekindled. Only gradually the outside starts to creep in and you go back to 'normal.' Then either you learn that this moment can be eternal or you forget again. Then hearts are broken, because the memory couldn't be sustained. When can it be sustained? When the memory is established in being, and when who you are is experienced here and now. Then the memory is constant, an eternal blissful memory that is not dependent on what other people say, do or remember. Only human beings who maintain this memory can keep the flame burning for eternity, can continue meeting again and again for the sheer pleasure of reliving this memory. They burst out together from infinity into the experience of enjoying the bliss of Life, the tingling of Light.

If you are impatient you are pushing that opportunity away. If you are impatient you are creating situations for yourself that are just the faded replica of what you really want. If you are impatient you announce to the universe, "I am not trusting." You announce, "I am not fully alive, because I didn't meet the one who will bring me life." You live your life as if you are missing something. You live your life as if life doesn't occur for you. You exclude yourself from life. Only when you live your life, will you have Life. If you don't like your life, change it. It's all in your hands. This is My call to you--change it. Don't settle for what is less than your perfection. Don't settle for what is less than bliss.

How do you reach perfection and bliss? Not by chasing after them. The more you chase, the farther away they go. How do you reach perfection and bliss? By accepting, by believing, by Understanding that there is more. This 'more' is your perfection. What you are looking for is all inside you, here and now. This 'more' is You. Turn your face to It.

*In our life we constantly have changes and challenges. How do we stay rooted in our bliss without being overshadowed by them?*

Life indeed is constant change. This adds to the beauty of life. By Law, life is change, flowing through the infinite replenishing ocean that constantly provides energy for the change. This principle of replenishment plays a role in every aspect of creation. Look at a tree, constantly changing. Every day the tree is slightly different. From where does the tree draw its life force to go through those changes?

Your life, too, is constantly changing. When you think of yourself as the leaf or the tree, you are first green and fresh, after a while you get darker, some insects bite into you, you turn brownish, you fall to the ground and slowly you disappear. Where is that leaf? It's gone. What happened to it? There is some speculation that it becomes fertilizer. From the perspective of that leaf which is attached to its appearance, to the illusion that it always has to stay green and fresh, its life is gone forever. The leaf forgot where it came from, and what gave it the ability to be fresh and green in the first place.

It's the same with human beings. The changes are always there for you to experience, to embrace, to own and then move on. And what helps you to move on and remain yourself, is the replenishing force inside you which even in the face of changes, will always exist.

What is this replenishing force I am talking about? It is this bottomless Energy, this enormous essence that is in you and never changes. It's always there to support you, giving rise to a new you. This is the Tree of Life that the Bible speaks about. Some call it Life, Being. What you call it doesn't matter. What does matter is that you always need to be firmly established in knowing that you come from that essence, that nothing in the world can shake you from it. You can go in and out, in and out, but you can never release yourself from It. You will never be dropped or lost. It's just a game on the surface where things change--shapes, colors, people you meet, situations--all change. Once you were fresh and green and one day you might be brown and all broken and eaten, but this is just on the surface. The eternal You will reveal Itself again and again. I find it very fascinating that this is hard for so many people to understand, while it is the very essence of their existence. Why is it so easy for so many of you to forget? Remember that changes and obstacles are just a little game on the surface, and no matter what happens, no one in the world can touch your essence, because your essence is God Itself, Himself, Herself. Do you think you could have a greater and stronger friend? So why worry? It's easy to find your point of balance, to remain unshaken in the face of what you call reality. Yes, sometimes the changes are unpleasant and you get bitten here and there, but this is just a game on the surface.

Remember that your purpose is not out there. Your purpose will unfold for you in your own inner journey toward perfection, in realizing the Source that you come from. You will find many clues to help you on this journey. Nothing is a coincidence. While you embrace everything that has happened, I am calling you to stay crystal clear and remain conscious, at every moment, of what you are striving for. The shortest way to your goal is to always desire Me, always see Me in everything you do and in everyone you meet. Ultimately, I want you to see Me in your Heart, and become Me. Is it clearer now?

*Yes, thank You.*

It is a very wonderful life that you are living. You are on a path of blissful discovery. Appreciate every moment of your life. Appreciate it because you deserve every bit of it and more. Don't ever settle for limitations, for less. This is My desire for you. Have a blissful day.

September 1, 1996

## 9

## Economy Springs From Fullness

Today's message is about business. Your world of business involves a specific kind of awareness. I call it world because when a person is doing business, or thinks he is doing business, he enters a certain mode, a certain awareness. People even say that business and pleasure don't mix. Most people believe that once they put on a suit and tie, or any other kind of uniform they use when they enter the world of business, they turn into a somewhat different person. They think they have to shift the way they regard others and the way they behave and radiate to the 'outside world.' When entering the world of business, most people put on masks to shield themselves and to hide the real person behind the mask. If they are stingy, mean and unfriendly in their personal life, they put on a mask of friendliness and generosity, in order to create trust. But if people are naturally kind, sharing, generous and tend to be trusting, they feel that this is not always good equipment in the world of business, and they put on a mask of toughness. These examples express the idea that you have different rules for the business world and regard it as different from your personal world. I am not here to blame or punish you for misbehaving. I'm here to reflect to you your own game.

Every minute of your life presents you with evidence of opposites. You observe those opposites and function accordingly. In the world of business you tend to use the tools you were given to manipulate what you observe, to win the game. Your motive is to overcome, to override, to outsmart.

Now, why is this so? It comes from the mistaken understanding of the nature of money, and of the Law of change. In business, people do not allow themselves to be who they really are. As a result, they have a tendency to separate spirit from matter, pleasure from business, generosity from efficiency, kindness from money-making.

If I were you, I would first find in myself a basic understanding of my desire to do business and would examine who in me wants to do business and why. I would ask myself why I'm taking this specific course in life. Then, when I'm very clear about the nature of my choice, I would proceed, taking mySelf with me. Since I'm taking mySelf with me, I am safe wherever I go. I don't need masks, I don't need weapons. What else can I take with me? The desire to be successful, to have more money, to excel, to be useful to society and to bring prosperity to myself, my family and my community. Now that I have piled all my desires for my business into my suitcase, I also want to take some basic understanding of the nature of economy, money and business.

Economy is the trading of resources, in an effort to increase and multiply them for the benefit of all participants. In other words, economy springs from fullness. The resources are there, and they are moved around from one community to another, from one place to another, from one kind of matter to a different kind of matter, from one state of existence to another. It's a distribution of what is, in a way that benefits all.

Now where does money come in? Money is the energy that helps you flow and distribute resources from one place to another. It's the magnetic force that pulls and connects things. Since money is energy that helps to match and connect, it cannot be stored and locked away in one place. It has to move and to flow; it is the connecting force. You could say it is the incentive.

In many periods of your history, some known to you and some not, distribution did take place without money. The trading of resources was exciting enough for human beings without incentives. But since some people developed an even stronger desire for prosperity, to the degree that they lost the belief in the fullness of what is, and developed the desire to accumulate more, the concept of money came about. Although the concept of money originated from lack, and in most cases served as a tool for unjust distribution, money, as an idea unattached to human intentions, is pure energy. It is the accumulated memory of money being misused that gave it a bad reputation. However, you can purify money by releasing yourself from the attached memory, and attach a new intention to it.

Money has no characteristics or consciousness. It is the consciousness of the beholder and producer of money that gives money its power. Since energy is something you cannot capture or hold in your fist, you cannot declare authority over it. Energy, in essence, truly belongs to all. It's the same with money. So take this understanding of money and add it to your suitcase. Now you are equipped with desires and understandings, and are ready to step into the world of business.

Whatever field you are in, you need to use everything you have in your suitcase. If you are a technician, and you forgot your tool-box, you cannot fix what you came to fix. You have to go home and bring your tool-box back with you. It's the same here. Without your clear desire and basic understanding, you cannot function in the business world and maintain happiness and success.

In this world there is a widespread belief in lack, a belief that there are not enough resources. You don't fully realize that you, with all your 'equipment,' are one of the main resources to contribute to and play in this game of economy. But when you understand that you come from a place of fullness to offer what you have and attract what you want, the result will be fullness. Giving, receiving--two poles-- energy flows, money flows. The result is success for both sides-- perfect economy. This is called successful business.

'Bad' business results when you forget your suitcase at home, when you forget to apply your understanding and clear desires. You forget to bring yourSelf into the game. Then you cling to other resources, like a child who imagines his father hitting the ball for him. Or, he finds solutions in cheating or accusing other players of cheating. When you don't come to the business world equipped with a clear understanding of your desires and of what money and economy are there for, you are relying on partial solutions. Some of them are very familiar--being suspicious, trying to accumulate without sharing, keeping it all at one pole, not letting it flow, not letting it be distributed. You give of yourself partially, afraid to share your fullness, believing that the less you give the more you have. This defies the Law of flow, of change. It defies the very definitions of economy, and of money as energy. Therefore it can only work sometimes to some degree. Then it will fall apart.

So if you are an unsuccessful businessman/woman, stop and check: are you coming from lack or from fullness? Are you in the world of business because you are worried about your mortgage, your bills? Are you in business because you want to accumulate for yourself? Are you afraid you won't have enough? Or are you there because you have a pure desire for prosperity and success for yourself and for your community? In the latter case you do understand the definitions of economy and of money, and you bring yourSelf to the game as the main resource. You bring with you not a worried, suspicious person, who believes in lack, but one who is well-equipped and willing to play the game.

How is all this connected to God is here and now? This brings Me back to the beginning of this message. It is when you believe that to enter business you have to step over into a different world, leaving all that is spiritual, philosophical and kind behind, that you make your first mistake. You create separation between who you are and what you are going to do in business. Functioning from separation is functioning from lack.

I tell you, you can find within you the capability to see wholeness in everything you do. You can flow in ever moving circles of life and achieve more. The exuberance, the enthusiasm of wholeness rolling, changing, moving, can be achieved only when all your roles are parts of wholeness--you as a father or mother, a businessman or businesswoman, a husband or wife and a friend--are one.

How can wholeness be achieved? By attuning to what you really want, knowing what moves you and knowing who you really are. In other words, you can attain oneness by keeping in touch with your innermost being, by being in touch with God within. When you come from within, there is wholeness in everything you do. Even when you face difficulties, you always have an anchor point. You can always come back to draw energy, guidance, understanding and strength to deal with a situation and move forward. Who you are dissolves difficulties. The more you cultivate wholeness in yourself, the less you face difficulties. If difficulties do manifest on your way, it's because your connection to wholeness is not complete yet. Success comes as a natural outcome of the full expression of wholeness.

*So our most important and highest business partner is our wholeness, or God within. Without this partner, we cannot succeed in business?*

Exactly. You might have an illusory experience of success to some degree, and this is what fools many people. But this success is very partial. The major question to ask yourself is, what *you* consider success.

*Can you please define what success in business is?*

Remember your suitcase, that you first filled with your pure desires. If your manifestation matches your desires, this is success. If the manifestation is partial, it's a partial success. Even if success seems obvious, one cannot judge the degree of success externally. Success is much more than just what you see.

*I am happy in my business and my employees are joyful and fulfilled. Is this automatically success?*

If it matches your desires, and the desires of everyone involved. Happiness and fulfillment are definitely good indicators of success.

*Regarding economic systems, we have communism, socialism and capitalism. What is the ideal economic system and how can we improve our system?*

The ideal economic system will naturally unfold when all people involved come from inner wholeness. Any economic system that is forced by government cannot be successful. It is clear that communism is not successful--what is manifested doesn't match the original desire, which was happiness and success for everyone. Moreover, the basic assumption of communism is that there is not enough for everyone to have a lot. Therefore, all need to share the little there is. This assumption comes from lack.

Socialism, even though it seems so fair, comes from the same basic assumption that there is not enough and not everyone can have what they want. Socialism is based on an innate mistrust in the natural distribution of resources that takes place when people are free to exercise their desire to share. What it tries to do is to patch and fix mistakes that were created previously by people who were holding on to their money, trying to control, and to accumulate what didn't belong to them. At the same time, others assume that they cannot create wealth for themselves. Instead of trusting in their natural right to have and their own power to manifest wealth for themselves, they believe that they don't have because wealth was taken away from them. Given this situation, governments created socialism, in an effort to fix the problem by taking from the rich and giving to the poor. In other words, government takes control of distribution rather than trusting nature's ability to distribute. As anything else that comes from mistrust in the process of life, it can be only partially successful. It can reach only so far, because it isn't in tune with the natural process.

Capitalism comes from the understanding that what you bring with you in your suitcase is the basis for what you get. Capitalism is just ignorant of what to put into the suitcase. It still lacks trust. Some people bring greed, cruelty or control, while others bring belief in lack, low self-esteem, or a sense of being a victim, so they go out and fail.

The perfect system would be based on the understanding that people do not need to take control but can trust the natural distribution of resources and regard themselves as one part in the flow of Energy, another resource among many. Coming from this understanding there is no need for a man-made system to manipulate and adjust economy. Economy will provide fullness and abundance, and it will function as it naturally needs to function.

*Is the new economy going to be on a national level or an international level? Should all the borders of nations and countries be opened? Or is it better to maintain national units of countries?*

Countries can remain as a very general frame or base for a community to define itself, to create pride and a sense of community achievement. But countries will shift from competition to cooperation. You find the first signs of this in the last 30 years or so. There is much room for improvement. Nationalism is a positive force if it leads to greater desires, if it leads you to a fuller self-expression of who you are as an individual and as a community. But while you function as a community or as a nation in order to fully express your uniqueness, you need to accept other nations in their uniqueness, and allow them to express their uniqueness as well. Then, from two unique units sharing their resources, their culture, their achievements in many areas of life, wholeness springs forth again. Wholeness, by definition, includes many parts that are connected to one center. This center is not a control center; therefore the diversity of the parts just adds to the wholeness, makes it more glorious, more whole.

September 2, 1996

## 10

## Beyond Time

Time is the span of vastness that stretches from one point in your awareness to another. Time is a man-made concept that exists on the border between given data and created data. You as humans have the feeling that you were born into a defined time concept, that was given as part of creation. Therefore you adopted it as one of the most fundamental laws of your existence. You adopted it so well that you arranged your whole life according to it. From the beginning of your history you took time for granted just as you took the rain, the sun, the moon and the gods of nature for granted. In other words, you became servants of time, for no other reason than not knowing better, or not remembering differently.

Time is probably the most ancient man-made concept. You even wove it into your story of creation. Since it is an integral part of your DNA, passed down over the generations, you cannot, even in your wildest imagination, conceive of an existence beyond time. What makes it harder on the individual level is that you are part of the mass consciousness. Since time is common among all civilizations, you never developed an independent attitude to question its existence. This is probably the most difficult pattern of thinking to change. Indeed there is no urgent reason to change it. Nothing really depends on it. It is not a prerequisite for enlightenment, for ideal living. Rather, it is an outcome. A society that will achieve ideal living will also reverse its slavery to the concept of time. So the question that remains for now is how to adapt to this concept in the most comfortable way.

Your bodies, whether or not you are aware of it, are in tune with the rhythm of nature. You call it 'biological clock.' Your bodies, with their own intelligence, know the genetic code of each moment of your existence in reference to the position of the stars, the moon, the sun, and to weather conditions. Your senses give you information which is translated in your brain into discriminative action to protect or assist the body. The body and the mind cooperate as a well-oiled machine in adapting to the outer world.

Your sensory system collects the data, processes it and helps you function in relation to the outer world. For example, the sensory system collects information about the rising and setting of the sun, about changing weather and changes that occur in nature. The process of discriminating and analyzing this data brings the body and mind to the conclusion that there is some time that elapses between one point in your awareness and another, that there is some movement. The mind and body sense the movement of energy in the ever-moving stream of Life as a gap, and this gap is translated as time.

This understanding of time would be just fine if you didn't involve your emotions and your thoughts in a judgmental way. If you didn't interpret the data that's collected, the impression of this information really wouldn't make any difference in your physiology and the way you function. What makes a difference is your interpretation of the information that your body and mind collect.

When your mind interprets change observed by the body as negative, the emotion that follows this thought is unpleasant, and the whole impression is registered and stored in your subconscious as such. If your mind interprets an observed change as positive, your emotions react accordingly and this information is stored in the subconscious as such. Every moment of your life you store either positive or not so positive impressions, and they build up and become who you think you are. This is the meaning of 'You are the creator of your own experience. You are what you think.' If the collective impression that you carry with you is of one kind, that's how you function, and that is why you bring yourself into situation A and not situation B. You find yourself doing certain things rather than others based on the accumulated interpretations of what your body observed.

By now you know that beyond the body, mind and emotions, there is more of you. The question is what role this 'more of you' plays in the big picture of your existence. The 'more of you' begins in your intuition. Your intuition leads you to inner guidance. This guidance comes from absolute stillness that resides in the innermost compartment of your Heart. That innermost compartment is who you are. Some people call it soul. Some call it God within. This Heart awareness, which is more than your thoughts, your body, your emotions, and everything else that you recognize as you, is free. It doesn't abide by earthly laws. It is not attached to anything. It has no outer reference point. It does not begin and does not end. Therefore, *it is beyond time.* So if you could live, do what you do, and maintain the connection with this 'free part of you' the experience of your life would be utterly different.

This inner awareness is like having another opinion, another vote in the supreme court, which comes from a different experience, a different awareness. This additional vote, in essence, is more powerful than all other votes. It is the supreme judge. This judge doesn't push, doesn't shout, but sits very quietly and speaks only when asked. This judge speaks very softly. You can hear him only when you are absolutely silent, only when you stop screaming, shouting and arguing. When you become very still, you hear him. You hear words of wisdom and you know he is right. Then, naturally the decision of what to do will change or will have a different flavor. A person who follows his inner guidance lives in wholeness. Living in wholeness means living who you really are, living life without mistakes, living in the flow, abiding by the Law of life.

What does this all have to do with time? The mistake that happens when you don't include the wiser part of yourself manifests in your interpretation of time. You consider the naturally occurring synchronization of your body with the outer signs that nature gives as a force that controls your life. Instead of rejoicing and merging into synchronicity with nature, you resist it, fight it, worry about it. Sometimes you even try to manipulate it. But if you let yourself surrender to the flow of nature's cycles and impulses, you become a master. The joy produced from being in synchrony with nature is a million times greater than the joy produced from manipulating it. In the experience of this joy, you naturally interpret the body's observation of the passage of time in a more positive way. Your emotions react accordingly, and the impressions on your subconscious will be positive. When the subconscious rejoices and is positive, there is no reason for the eruption of disease, aging, and decrease of energy.

For example, let's take a day when you surrender to nature. You naturally wake up with the sunrise, you are in tune with your body, eat when and what is best for the body, and you retire after sunset. In this case, you let the body do what it remembers very well--be synchronized with nature. This can happen not only during a day but by synchronizing to the moon and the stars, also during a month. The impressions that the body will collect from the surroundings will be much more pleasant. This, in turn, will influence your thoughts, emotions, the subconscious, and will reverberate and reflect on your inner being and create wholeness. Now you will draw from your inner being the strength of stillness, freedom and eternity. You will saturate your emotions and your thoughts in this stillness. Your body naturally comes in tune with the flow and reacts accordingly. Then your interpretations will be more positive. It is a never ending cycle.

But what you do is try to master time with your mind. You try to outsmart time; you ignore the signals that nature gives. You ignore your part in this wholeness. You consider yourself as a separate unit that functions by itself, rather than an important part in a bigger picture, in which each contributes to wholeness.

Needless to say, when many people synchronize with the cycles of nature, it will bring about a change. In doing so, you develop trust in the wisdom of the natural rhythm, and you lose interest in manipulating it. The nature of your observation changes as well, and therefore the nature of your decisions and your emotions changes. As a whole, you become a positive society that is in tune with the inner being, connected to God within, having trust in the wholeness of it all. Then it is easy to see God in everyone. It's easy to know how you fit in the big picture. It's easy to know who you are and what you are here for. It's naturally easy to make the right decisions, and it is easy to see the beauty in this tremendous, awesome Creation. Then it is easy to accept, believe and know that God is here and now.

September 3, 1996

## 11

## Make God Your Religion, for a Change

Today's message is how to incorporate religion in your life. What is the importance of the path? Where does the path begin and where does it lead? How do you know you are on the path? What is the goal in following a path in the first place? Today I am going to touch on many painful points. I'm going to shake many fundamental beliefs and turn things upside down. To begin with--religion has caused more damage in world affairs, physical and non-physical, than many wars or individual misconduct.

Without exception, people who have come to know Me intimately, and brought my plea, my truth into public awareness, didn't originally intend or were not guided to create a religion. Without exception, the knowledge that was cognized at different times and in different places around the globe brought out the same truth. This knowledge was put into context, language, color and shape, according to the earthly manifestation and experience of the messenger. Without exception, experiences like this were a pure merging of one's self with the Self; turning from outer faculties to experience the inner essence, and finally uniting with It. In those moments of merging and realization the only desire was to Be.

When one emerges from such an experience, one is transformed. This transformation occurs as a natural outcome of the experience. It also occurs in order for people in the physical surroundings to observe the transformation and recognize it as a reflection of their own inner truth. The visible transformation is there to stimulate the same experience in other people.

In this process two things may happen. First, the person himself, coming out of the inner to communicate with the outer, becomes attached to the experience. As he moves farther from the seed of the experience, he becomes convinced that it is a once-in-a-lifetime event, unique to himself. In this attachment he puts the experience into a framework that is passed on as the only possibility of experiencing God. The second and more common thing that occurs when the transformation is shared with others, is their misinterpretation and misunderstanding due to the fact that they didn't have the experience. Then they attempt to capture the experience in words, rules, and a single way of life.

While the realized person is still in physical form, the people around him can maintain the innocence of the experience to some degree. But the farther the message is passed on in time and space, the more it loses its purity and innocence, and the more it becomes fixed and attached to the human understanding of the current time and place.

An experience of uniting with God is not a religious experience. Religion begins somewhere later in this process. The stronger the followers are, the greater the chance that the pure message will be turned into a fixed religion. The seed of all religions is the same, however each flower is different, depending on the soil, the sun, the rain, and people's love and attention to the flower.

What happened to the different flowers? Does religion serve its sole purpose, which is to bring this experience of God into many people's hearts? All religions have moved away from the seed, but nevertheless they still maintain the essence of the seed. All religions have moved farther from their ability to achieve their own defined goal. Religion, as a set of rules, customs, guidelines, sayings and interpretations, succeeded in keeping people in a frame, a social frame, a frame of thoughts and a frame of behavior. It helped people to stay in the context of their community--a blessed activity in itself-- but is that the fulfillment of the goal? In the name of religion people often managed to distort the original teachings completely, as is well known in your history.

Who are the people who, from within their religion, *did* manage to enliven the seed, to recapture fragments of the original experience? They are people who maintained the flame burning in their heart, people who truly desired to achieve the original goal of their religion. They may have used the outer shell of the religion, but the experience in their heart had no name, no color, no shape.

There is no one religion that leads you better, or in a shorter way, to the experience of uniting with God. The same goes for different paths. Many paths maintain themselves in the framework of religions. Others leave this framework, because many people have realized how inadequate religion is when it loses its orientation toward the goal. In a desperate attempt to fill the void, many paths were adopted.

I do not make any judgment or recommendation regarding religions and paths. There is no one right way, and any attempt to judge right from wrong is derived solely from one's ego and desire to influence and control. I am telling you today that all ways are good. You want to fast at the top of the Himalayas? Good. You want to run on the beach for the rest of your life? Good. You want to devote yourself to God's life in a convent or an ashram? Good. You want to be a householder and have many children? Good. You want to be a devotee of a guru and devote your life to service? Good. You want to be a successful businessman, artist, dancer, healer? Good. You don't want any of these? Good.

There is no set of values according to which you are judged, weighed, catalogued. This is all your creation. Do what you want to do, do what gives you joy. This is My only recommendation. But for God's sake, desire Me. For God's sake, while you continue to develop, enlighten yourself, enrich yourself, contribute to your community, be fit, be healthy, be successful, be famous, be unknown, be poetic, be smart, put your Beingness before all that. Because the art, the healing, the success, the wisdom--all of these come from Being.

Make Being your religion.

Make Me, for a change, your religion.

And when you utter the name of God in your prayers

be sure that you experience, you vibrate the name of God.

When you utter the name of God during your services,

be sure to burn in His light.

Be sure to make it your most intimate experience,

and then go and become whatever you want.

This is the ultimate religion.

Nothing else is needed,

because everything else will come without you even trying.

*You say, desire Me, or keep a flame in your heart. Can you talk about how to do it? What is the right way to accomplish this fullness in devotion and in prayer?*

The devotional path is a most popular one, because by nature human beings like to express what's in their hearts. In their daily life people are restrained and very cautious about that, but during a segment of devotional activity, they allow themselves to feel what is in their heart. This is one of the main reasons why religions survive and flourish. They give an outlet to this burning desire, this burning feeling of devotion in the heart.

When I appeal to people to keep this flame burning, it is a very familiar concept to many. It is more common among women because of the misconceptions regarding the expression of manhood, and the values that your society developed regarding what's appropriate for a man and what's not. Nevertheless, recently more and more men have been attracted to the devotional path. More and more men are yearning to express what's in their hearts. More and more people in general recognize the contribution that the heart makes to their life. Therefore, I appeal first to those who already have this experience, or who are inclined to experience it. I want to make it clear for them that by keeping the flame burning in their heart, they are experiencing exactly what was intended.

Now I am appealing to all people who are seeking answers and exploring many possibilities in the spiritual realm. I remind them that no matter what they choose to do, this returning to the heart, this simple act that doesn't require money, equipment, teachers, or workshops, is what is important. Just this simple turning in to the heart, keeping this flame burning, pulsating, is what will bring them peace and blessings. This is their strength, this is the seed from which all flowers can blossom.

I understand it is a challenge to maintain awareness of the flame in your heart while living your daily life. But at the same time, My simple request to turn to the heart doesn't present any threat, complications or expectations. It can open doors for those who desire and search for more.

How can you do it? There is no doing involved. Just a willingness to set aside all concepts, all knowledge, all theories, all desires to be right, all desires to prove others wrong. A willingness to consider a different possibility. This willingness is not threatening. It does not require giving up anything. It is easy to incorporate into any lifestyle, in any community. The willingness to consider the existence of something more than the immediate reality is the only thing that is needed to find God within. This willingness will be amplified and helped in so many ways and by so many 'coincidences' that there will be no question of what to do and how to do it--it will be self evident. It will be the most intimate and personal experience, but at the same time, obvious to everyone. From this experience shared by everyone, a new kind of society will spring up, with new motivations and new directions. There will be no need to discuss the experience, to evaluate or prove it, because there will be nothing to prove. Spontaneously, activity will be guided by the desire for good, by the Law of ever-moving, ever-changing--the Law of life.

*Is it better for people who left the churches and temples to come back and bring these qualities back to their churches, or can people stay in their small circles, in the family or on the individual level?*

Any way the desire for more devotional experience is expressed is blessed. By living the Law people won't feel the necessity to prove anyone wrong, or to overrule or overcome. All mosques and churches, synagogues and temples can coexist. There will be a temporary stage of development, when a surge of devotional experience will be expressed. More religions may pop up, because there will be a need for additional avenues of devotional expression. In time this surge, this need, will subside, because life will be devotion. This is the Golden Age to which the prophets refer-- people living with God. Thus all of life will be an expression of appreciation. The need for the diversity of religions will give way to deep understanding of the oneness of this Force, in which everyone is riding as in a chariot. This understanding, this knowingness, will be so apparent that everyone will live in oneness. The idea 'the world is my family' will become a reality. Because if you share a most intimate experience with someone, what could bring you closer than that? The need to protect feelings and the fear to express them will be dropped, guardedness will no longer be necessary.

*Are we going to see more flexibility and openness to change, expressed by the leaders of various religions?*

There is no need to expect anything from anyone. Everyone will be part of the change.

*Will the change start from the inner desire of each one of us?*

Yes, but it will spread like wildfire. The barriers will fall down.

*Are we already in this process, or is it coming?*

You are already in the initial stages of it. There are many people who already carry this seed, this burning flame in their heart.

*So we are looking to a future in which religions will complete their cycle, their need to exist, and they will dissolve into life?*

Yes, because the main reason for the establishment of religions will disappear. This process began in the last few centuries, when people moved away from religion, but many still have not found a substitute.

*You mentioned that even the great teachers, the prophets, made mistakes when they transmitted their experiences to the masses, even to their disciples. I can see that it would happen in the generations after the teachers, but I have difficulty seeing these great teachers making mistakes.*

You human beings, have a tendency to make holy, and therefore untouched, anything that you associate with God. You make it so holy that you create a gap between you and what's God. You introduce fear. You introduce separation. The fundamental understanding is that there is a most holy, infinite eternal aspect, which permeates everything. Everything that springs out of this very holy center carries within it the seed of holiness. But in the process of coming out into diversity, multiple possibilities, infinite variations happen. None of them are mistakes, but things happen and they sometimes deviate from perfection. This is all right. It's part of the process. The holiness is not lost. It's just forgotten, or not allowed to be expressed fully. It is always there.

Therefore, even great teachers deeply saturated with holiness, in the process of delivering their message to the world, might deviate from perfection. There is no mistake in it. It is just there. The more the person is saturated with holiness, the more fully he lives in the flow, the more dramatically he experiences any deviation from perfection, because the deviation seems so foreign to the experience of who he really is. The consequences of his experience of this slight 'falling' are more evident, because they are in sharp contrast to who he is. For the majority of people whose life is an accumulation of mixed experiences, some in the flow and most not, the contrast is not so evident.

It's harder for most of you to identify the so-called mistake, and bring all your experiences back to the flow. It is for this reason that all the masters, founders of religions and path-makers, came to help you to release your so-called mistakes, to return, to unite in the flow, to be wholly saturated, permeated by holiness, to be a child of God, as you call it. In this huge range of possible experiences you can find numerous degrees of holiness. Although you can make an effort to release the 'mistakes', one by one, particle by particle, a task that may take many lifetimes, you can just sweep them all together and join the flow, in a blink of an eye. You understand that this way of speaking about degrees of holiness, is an effort on My side to adapt Myself to your way of thinking, that measures and compares everything. From My perspective, no matter where a person is on this scale, he is perfect.

*Can you briefly describe the goal for our generation regarding religions and knowing God?*

The goal is to find the kingdom of heaven within. How? By keeping this flame burning in your heart. When Jesus said: 'I am a child of God,' they made Him holy and themselves unholy. He came to say what I am saying in this message--everyone is a child of God. Jesus was not the only one who said that the kingdom of heaven is within. Look at other scriptures. There are numerous descriptions of the inner temple of the heart. What do people do? They turn to elaborate temples, rather than turning within, to their intimate 'inner temple.' There is nothing wrong with temples. I admire your beautiful buildings, but I reside in the temple of your heart.

September 4, 1996

## 12

## The Well of Life

Your body continues presenting itself to you, demanding attention, calling for satisfaction. Your mind continues, busy as ever, asking questions, wondering, looking backward and forward. But something completely different is emerging--different desires, an inner strength. What you would like to do now is to draw from this inner strength and empower yourself. This inner strength is undefinable, unexplainable. It is not dependent on nutrition, sleep, support, weather, or mood. It is absolutely unchangeable, steady, and always there. This is what I want you all to bring out to the surface. Turn this very thing, that has no name, into the master of your life, the one and only one that dominates your life.

The harder the external reality seems to be, the more magnificent the effect of your inner strength in your life will be. The harder the external life seems to be, the easier it is to delve into your inner Well and draw from its strength. This is the foundation from which miracles spring. I am calling on you to disregard the ease or difficulty, the blessings or hardships. The Well is always there, no matter what. Whether it rains, or there is a drought, this Well is always bubbling with water. You can come to it in days of lack or in days of abundance.

In fact, just come *from* it rather than come *to* it. And if you come from it, all your days will be watered. This is the true meaning of God is here and now. Don't wait for the drought to look for the Well. Don't wait for the crisis to find miracles. You cannot count on the changing surface of your life, but you can always count on the Well. Turn the Well into the source of everything you do. Draw from it constantly. Then you will find your life less influenced by changes. You will find that there is always water for your needs.

This is a fundamental principle of life. This is a recipe for happiness. Aren't you always looking for recipes for a healthy life, for fitness, happiness, success? I am giving you the ultimate recipe.

You see, the Source always exists, and limitations are experienced only in your limited reality. Recognize the fluctuations in your external life but stop being afraid of them. Realize that in order to experience joyfully a continuous flow in your physical life, you first have to establish the experience of an inner flow, in what you call spiritual life. Your outer blessings are always a reflection of your inner strength. If this inner drawing from the Well, were established in the heart and the awareness of every politician, scientist, physician, teacher, farmer and everybody else, then the outer flow would be ever-growing.

A society that experiences alternate states of abundance and lack, progress and its opposite needs enough people who lead with inner strength, drawing from the Well, staying in the flow. Then there is progress. But when fear takes over, trust is crushed. Too many believe that success is their own creation and forget where the water comes from. Then the whole society moves backward. Suddenly the buckets seem to be the source. You fluctuate in your political and economic life, between great successes and much fear, between prosperity and poverty. You don't seem to be able to establish a golden age in which all humanity progresses. Rather, you are functioning on the surface, like waves that go up and down, up and down.

My call to you is, stop where you are for a moment. Climb up an invisible ladder, and view what is around you. Do you like what you see? Would you like it to be better, more glorious? Would you like everyone to enjoy prosperity? Would you like everyone to enjoy the fruits of life and experience joy in this short-term physical experience? Would you like everyone to experience abundance?

Would you like to live in a world where people naturally maintain their life with dignity?

Stop fixing society. You cannot fix anything unless you water yourself with the water from the Well. How do you do that? By coming back to Me. Not tomorrow, not after other people do, not after you see a change, not when you are sick. Now, where you are right now, rich or poor, free or captive, busy or bored--it doesn't matter. Find Me inside you. Find inside you the one who is not your mind, is not your senses, is not your job, is not your friends, is not your success or failure. Find the Well within you. Once and for all 'turn on the switch' for eternal supply, so you will never again have to depend on outside switches; never again have to fear that the flow of your life will stop.

There are many paths that lead to the Well. By no means try to set rules for how to reach this Well. Don't try to tell anyone that their path is longer or shorter. Just get there in your own way and rejoice when you meet others. The inner happiness you draw will be so overwhelming that anything else you regarded as so important will be secondary. New energy will be awakened inside you that you never dreamed of before. From this overwhelming joy that you will experience within and see in the eyes and hearts of everyone around you, you'll create your Golden Age.

September 5, 1996

## 13

## Sex is a Divine Experience

Good morning. We are here together on this glorious day for another adventure. Today's topic will be love and sex. Good topic, huh! So many of you find it very interesting but still regard it with a distorted outlook. Love and Sex are the same in the sense that they are both energies.

Love stands at the basis of your existence because it is the very thing that creates you and constitutes you. Love is found on your cellular level, and on your atomic level. Love is the force that springs out of stillness into action; it is the original thought that creates you. You see, Love is the foundation for your existence.

As long as you were nonphysical, sex was nonexistent. Sex facilitates Love into manifestation in the physical world. Sex was created exactly for this purpose--to clothe your loving consciousness with a physical expression. Now, you might think that love is all consciousness and sex is all physical, and this is the seed of your mistake. Sex is a facilitator for love, therefore, it cannot exist without love. The only reason for the existence of sex is love. There is no definite line where love ends and sex begins. Love and sex intermingle on the journey that begins with thought and ends with a physical manifestation.

Although you are inclined to believe that sex is the coming together of physical bodies, there is much more to it on different levels. Even in the animal world, love plays an important role in the process of multiplying the species. What is it if not Love, that is at the source of the desire to multiply and continue the process of creation? This is the life stream, the life force that never stops, ever creates.

Human beings were given a greater role in the play of consciousness and in the flow of creation. They were given the ability to consciously create and their understanding of love and sex is much broader and more complex. The misunderstanding of the connection between love and sex stems from the same mistake you make in any other area where you depart from oneness. All your physical functionings, including sex, were given to you for the experience of joy and oneness, and to ensure the continuity of your physical existence. Therefore, sex should be regarded with much appreciation, humility and reverence, just as you want to regard eating, taking care of your physical health and even praying. You want to do all these with love.

Nevertheless, you do have more participating emotions and feelings in the area of sex. Why? For a very good reason: because this is when you most experience the intensity of love and get closer to the experience of oneness, closer to God. Sex is the most natural way in which human beings can focus their energy on love and experience joy at the same time. In other areas of life one needs to interact more consciously, one needs to intend more, it doesn't come as easily.

When in your history male energy took over, the desire for control developed. Everything possible was done to control sexual experience, just as everything was done to control the spontaneous experience of God. In order to manipulate these essential experiences of concentrated love, male energy tried to control female energy. This desire for control came from fear and it is deeply embedded in your subconscious. From this desire to control, all the rules about what's right and wrong, all the interpretations about what is allowed and what is not, what is natural and what is not, what is shameful and what is not, were established. Therefore, as a society you have grown to feel ashamed and embarrassed in the arena of sex.

In recent time, in order to come out of this unpleasant situation, many human beings have been rebelling, bringing sex out of hiding into the light. Still the understanding remains distorted and sex is taken out of wholeness.

Now let's all relax and go back to the original Law of the universe--the Law of oneness, the Law by which everything operates--like attracts like. If you have a feeling of love, you are drawn to everything that embodies love. And if you are both vibrating love, at that moment you are one. If you are one you have the freedom to express your oneness in any way you desire.

It's as simple as that. So aren't you alarmed? I just announced a sex revolution! Don't you have questions?

*In light of this understanding, are values such as marriage, family etc. still intact and important? If someone is a family member but has deep feelings for another person, can he express them? Or, by doing so will he act against his wholeness?*

The family is a divine creation. Men and women were created with the intention to unite and in their unity they facilitate another creation. The family unit is a creation of love and is therefore holy, divine and whole. If the family is maintained in wholeness, there won't be any desire to go out of this unity. When you experience unity, nothing in the world will take you away from it. It is when people come together for the wrong reasons that they are easily distracted, since they aren't experiencing unity.

Now, I do understand that when people turn away from God and do not abide by God's Law, society sees a need for structure, based on the belief that man-made laws would bring people back to unity. But look at your history, do man-made laws help? In most cases not. And if they appear to help outwardly, it's out of people's fear of what the society will say, what God will say, or fear of punishment--all the wrong reasons.

Furthermore, the moment that a sperm and an egg come together is mystical, unknown to you. When your scientists look at this phenomenon, they cannot understand what the senses cannot examine, monitor, measure. They cannot see the life force, the divinity, the light of the soul that comes in. What could be more divine than that moment? Many people did and do have the sense of it, and therefore have tried to structure in law the holiness of this moment. From this stems the concept of the holiness of marriage and the fight against divorce and abortion.

The understanding of the divinity of that moment is correct, but the way society goes about enforcing it is a another story. We are touching here on very delicate issues, such as the woman's freedom to choose her own destiny, the freedom to choose your own mate, the decision to cut life force from physical existence. Each one of these issues is important. I am telling you that rules wouldn't be necessary if human beings would allow
the flow of Love to direct their actions. Marriages would be holy by their nature, not by certificates. Life would come forth when intended with Love, and women would be protected naturally.

And how is it possible to bring this about, in such a complex world? By accepting, believing, and realizing that God is here and now, as the first premise of each action of your life.

*This acceptance will coordinate and adjust all actions spontaneously?*

Man-made laws will be dropped by the minute. They will be like old garments, not useful any more.

*How can we maintain holiness and purity in this area of life which includes pleasure and temptation?*

77

Balance. It is like food you eat as an attempt to fill some emptiness, rather than having the pure intention of nourishing the body. Most sex in the world today is an attempt to fill emptiness, seeking pleasure as meaning for existence, rather than summoning love. I have nothing against pleasure. Sex was designed to bring joy, just as the worship of God is a joyful experience. New life should come with joy and pleasure, like a beautiful dance. But it has all become distorted and taken out of proportion. Now I know you have another question.

*Is it all right to have sex only for the pleasure?*

Of course it is. I'm not here to tell you what's right and what's not right. The desire of two to express their love through physical union is also a kind of worship of God. If this is a union of vibration that says, love, love, love, it means this is the shared desire of two souls, of two human beings to unite. They can find numerous ways to share the joy of their love. One of them is the pleasure of sex. Nothing is more beautiful than that. The angels are singing. But if you engage in sex in order to achieve something or to manipulate someone, the residue is tasteless. No music there. You separate sex from Love.

Sex is a beautiful expression of knowing oneself inwardly. When young, and focused mainly on the physical manifestation of the being, sex will be expressed one way. As you develop your consciousness and become more aware of your wholeness, this awareness will be reflected in the desire for sex and in its expression. If one's desire is to detach herself from sex altogether, and it comes as a natural desire which leads to more bliss--wonderful. It means that at that time this individual brings into the foreground of her awareness the focus of nonphysicality. It means that the intention of that soul in this lifetime was not for the propagation of the species, but for a different purpose. Therefore, the need for sex is absent. The person has awakened to her original intention. This doesn't imply that she is more developed than others who do experience sex. There is no value judgment here. Remember, sex is energy. Sex is not in the category of less spiritual development. So those who tell you that to develop spiritually you have to exclude sex, are mistaken. One cannot generalize, one cannot control others' vibrations. It's the inner awakening to who you are that determines your path.

When you are awakened to the deeper meaning of who you are, and why you are here, you know spontaneously what to do, how to be without mistakes, without suffering. Everything flows beautifully, everyone plays their own note in this glorious symphony.

*When You speak about our ability to fulfill our desires, does it include sexual desires?*

Yes, it includes sexual desires, but the question is, what is your understanding of 'sex' and 'desire'? Sex is a big taboo in your society. Nevertheless it was given to you to be used when your feelings lead you to it. When I say feelings, I don't mean lust, or bodily desires. I'm talking about deep emotions that come from the heart. When you come from this deep place you can do nothing wrong. When you are really in touch with yourself, you know very clearly how to differentiate between bodily desires and heart desires. You find people saying, "I really want sex and I need it right now." This is what I call bodily desires, which are often influenced by magazines, movies, etc. You are led to believe they are your desires.

When you truly love someone, the desire to have a sexual relationship is natural. From this level of loving when both of you are whole, and you understand that the basis for any relationship is the wholeness of its participants, then this uniting is a wonderful and divine experience . But sex is not the only way of uniting. Two can unite physically and still be far apart and they can unite without physically touching each other. When the awareness of oneness is flavored by the sexual experience, it is like a beautiful offering to the Divine.

*What role does physical beauty play in influencing relationships? Can I trust my attraction based on the person's physical beauty or am I excluding possibilities because of that?*

Beauty can change from moment to moment. Beauty is real and unreal at the same time. It is like standing in front of a beautiful Van Gogh painting. Your feelings respond to it. When you stand in front of this picture, what kind of feelings do you have? You feel attracted, you are in awe, you are curious, you may even be a little bit in love. Then you move to another picture and a different set of feelings come to you. When you explore your feelings you find out that many other feelings are interwoven, which lead you to new discoveries about yourself and others. There is not only one way to look at beauty.

Beauty is a gift I gave Earth and there is beauty in everything I created. So, if you want to know if beauty has a role in relationship, of course it does, although not necessarily the way you understand it now. You will learn to identify and be attracted to inner beauty and then your concept of beauty will change. You might even find yourself attracted to people you didn't consider beautiful before. Be careful in judgment. When you identify people as beautiful or not, there is a lot of judgment. Judgment is a faculty of your mind. Let your heart lead you. Let your heart sense the energies that flow from a person and feel how those energies intermingle between the two of you. Let the heart be your eyes. You can even close your eyes, and when you open them with the approval of the heart, beauty will stand before you. It won't necessarily be the beauty of a model in a magazine or a commercial.

*Can you explain whether it is a good idea for a man while expressing love physically, to avoid ejaculating in order to transmute his sexual energy to spiritual energy?*

Sex or the absence of sex doesn't guarantee spiritual achievement. There is nothing holy or unholy in sex. There are infinite things that you do during the day, that are as important and essential to your being as sex, and you don't make a fuss about them. Regarding your question, I am not going to recommend anything that might be misinterpreted as the only way. Enough bibles have been written, and many of you believe if you don't follow them you will die and go to hell, or you'll fall off the path. All these are expressions of fear. Do just this one simple thing--always be connected to your Heart, to the Source. Then naturally you'll know what to do.

Regarding your specific question, a man's ability to control ejaculation is a beautiful manifestation of his ability to master his physicality, to use the body as a tool rather than being controlled by it. It is a beautiful manifestation of one's ability to choose a different awareness in the midst of physicality.

Sex is energy. Like any other aspect of life, it comes first from wholeness. It moves you from one awareness to another. It moves your whole species from one awareness to another. Sex is My own little patent for your existence in this physical world. Your existence in this world originates from consciousness. Sex is not excluded from it.

What you do in the details of the sex act goes back to your own choice every moment of your life: how you regard your body, how you regard your beingness in relation to sex, how you regard the other person's body and the other person's beingness in relation to sex. When two beings have the broader understanding that they are connected, the outcome will be beautiful, like everything else in life which springs from oneness. But if they focus exclusively on their physicality, the relationship will not last. Therefore the details are

81

very secondary. There is no one way that is allowed or not allowed. Whatever you are able to do during the sex act is all right, because you are able to do it. Whatever you can do with your body is yours, as a gift.

October 25, 1995
September 6, 1996

## 14

## Love and Health

Health is a very popular topic, second only to sex. Why health? Because your body comes closest to what you conceive yourself to be. You believe that your body identifies who you are. If you like what you see, you're happy; if you don't like what you see, it makes you miserable. You judge by your eyes. If you like what you hear you are happy, if you don't like what you hear, it makes you uncomfortable. You judge by your ears. If you like what you eat, if it's tasty to you, you enjoy it; if it is not so tasty you spit it out. You judge by your sense of taste. If you touch something and it is pleasant, you like it, if it doesn't feel pleasant, you feel disgust. You judge by your sense of touch. If you smell a rose, you are blissful, if you smell bad smells, you run away. You judge by your sense of smell. In other words, you base your reality on what you see, hear, taste, touch. and smell.

You turn the sensory system into your ultimate guidance in life and absolutely accept and trust the data collected by it, feed it to your brain and act upon it. You take the data collected by your senses, strain it through your thinking process, feed the outcome to your heart, and base your feelings upon it. In other words, you shape your identity, what you believe yourself to be, according to a very limited perception. Since you operate from this limited perception, the final product can only be limited.

Furthermore, the information that you collect from the very moment you are born is stored and accumulated. Therefore, your behavior is based not only on what you perceive at a given moment, but also on what you have perceived from the moment you were born. Your perception is amplified, like interest compounded on a loan. You hear people say, "I'm good at this but not good at that. I can do this but I cannot do that. I hate that, cannot stand it, and I love this," etc. These convictions are based on the accumulated information that you processed and stored in the life span of your body. This storage happens in your subconscious. Every action performed by a human being is an expression of immediate conscious conclusions added to all the accumulated subconscious conclusions.

In this manner a person shapes what he thinks to be himself. Where in this shaping of identity do you integrate the possibility of 'something more?' Where in this becoming is something greater than the immediate context introduced? In your life when you feel stuck and unable to solve a problem, you invite an outside expert. You look for answers in different directions. Sometimes you introduce new insights and suddenly the whole problem dissolves. Where do you get this new insight? Where can you turn? Some people call it the sixth sense, which suggests the possibility that there is more to you than the five senses, the mind and the feelings; more than the tools that serve you so obviously in life. Here I am referring to the inner world, the faculties that are not so obvious. In the process of becoming it will be most fruitful for you to feed yourself not only from outside impressions but also from the innermost faculties, which are connected to infinity, to the Source.

You'll agree with Me that by any logic the Source must contain within It all the information a person needs, because the Source carries within Itself the original intention, the blueprint of what is to become of you. More specifically, a person who can incorporate his intuition, who can turn to God-within, who can trust in the innate knowledge that he carries within, will be closer to the original intention, which is perfection.

Now, what does all this have to do with health and love? When using the word 'health' most people think of lack of health. You really regard health only when you confront its opposite. Dis-ease is an indication that something went wrong in collecting the data, processing it and creating the final product, which is you. Dis-ease is introducing some foreign element, which was invited based on incorrect interpretation or processing. It is based on accumulated memory of very partial data that came from your sensory system, was amplified in your subconscious and became your reality. If you can dissolve the memory and eliminate it at its seed form, you will eliminate dis-ease and regain health, which is the natural perfection that was intended in the first place.

Since your innate desire is to be perfection, to be health, you identify dis-ease as an enemy, an intruder, and you try to fight it, believing that if you fight it, it will somehow disappear. But by making it disappear on the surface, you really don't deal with its origin. The seed from which it manifested is still safely located where it was planted. In order to clear yourself of this intruder in a beneficial way, and for dis-ease to disappear completely you have to eradicate the seed from the system.

How would you do that? By inviting the expert from outside, which, in our case, is really the expert from inside. What can the expert from inside contribute, now that the dis-ease is manifest? How can your intuition--which leads to inner guidance, to God within--help, now that you already have this dis-ease? It will help to dissolve the seed and make it disappear. How can you dissolve the seed of dis-ease? By melting it with Love. By burning it with the fire of Love. Because only by burning it with the fire of Love, will the accumulated memory, which provided the seed with the necessary substance to grow, dissolve. The accumulated data, its interpretation over the years, and the feelings that followed, became the food for the seed to grow into illness, any kind of illness--physical, emotional, mental.

However, no matter how long ago the seed was planted and how much it was amplified, it can all be healed by the power of Love.

There is no force in the universe that can withstand the power of Love. Love can heal everything. Therefore you cannot introduce the concept of health without its counterpart, Love. They go together like a hand in a glove.

To make it even clearer, Love is energy. Love is a medicine which can clear and bring into balance every unbalanced situation. This energy, Love, can be translated and expressed in many ways. By no means is it the expression, "I love you" which really has no meaning. Love is expressed in the healing power of a plant, of a healer, of sound, of light, of crystals, of smells, of air, of nature. All of it is saturated by Love. There is no existence without the energy of Love. Love is the Absolute that permeates everything.

How do you use this lofty Love energy that permeates everything? By focusing it. By intending it and by letting it happen. How do you do this? By inviting that 'outside expert,' by believing that there is something beyond your reality, something more than the final 'product' that you created for yourself. This final 'product' includes: your physicians, your exercises, your set of limitations of what's possible, your beliefs that this is life and there is nothing more to it, your beliefs as to who and what can help you, your beliefs that things are the way they are and nothing can change them. Let go of all this. Break out of your boundaries. Open up and allow yourself to introduce Love. Begin with loving yourself. Begin with forgiving yourself for all those things you've been told are your sins, your mistakes.

Turn over a new page, and start to process the data anew. Detach yourself from the accumulated memory that you have carried on your back for eons. Declare that you don't need it anymore. Declare that you are open to new possibilities. From this new awareness you can seek help, because now everything is possible. Even pain can be new, free of accumulated memories and attachments. Being new, the pain is not so dense, and you can let it go. Then any help you receive will be more effective. You can create a new 'womb,' but this time you create a 'womb' for the seed of health, not dis-ease. You can feed the seed with love, with a sense of freshness, of liberty, a sense of wonder, a sense of no limitations, a sense of all possibilities. And in this womb, any medicine you take, any method you introduce, any nourishment of Love, will contribute to the growth of the new seed.

The outcome will be health, perfection. There is nothing the body desires more than to come back to perfection. The body is designed to operate in perfection. Even if it is laden with layers of memory, of sickness, its innate desire, its innate power is to reach wholeness again. Under the layers of heavy memories, there remains the original memory of bliss, happiness, and wholeness. If you feed this original memory with Love you will amplify the sense of bliss and wholeness, and slowly cause the unpleasant memories to dissolve. You have access to the Well of all knowledge, all health, all possibilities. By loving yourself you can reach in and draw out that 'missing element,' that 'magic,' to nurture the original memory, and then the healing will unfold. Love yourself, because you are your best healer.

*Can you describe how Love energy can heal an organ?*

Energy works according to the Law of attraction--like attracts like. When, in the process of accumulating information, you introduce fear, self criticism, hate, anger, guilt, worry--elements which are also energy--they attract to themselves more and more of their own kind. These feelings grow and they become your reality. By the time dis-ease breaks out, it is just an outer physical expression of the energy that you, and only you, introduced to your system. Fortunately, the cells of your body that gave in under this heaviness still hold the memory of their Source, the intelligence to regenerate themselves and return to wholeness. They can do so at any moment of their existence, provided they are helped. When you introduce Love it will attract to itself the innate memory of your cells, which is Love, and together they will create wholeness. The help they need is an energy that is alike, an energy of Love. You are the one who introduced the 'negative' feelings. You are the one responsible to introduce 'positive' feelings. How can you do this? First by loving yourself, and then by allowing others to love you, opening to new possibilities of healing, allowing perfection to take place.

*What can one do when facing an acute situation?*

It's never too late to introduce Love, to open to new possibilities. Never too late to make a shift in your awareness, to cross the borderline of your limitations. Never too late to introduce trust that everything is possible. If it happens that you make the transition into a different dimension, your newly acquired state of allowing will make the transition easier and your next experience will start in a much more blissful way. Not only that, those around you, who are desperately trying to help you, will be left with a tremendous lesson to apply in their own life. The intelligence that created you is never lost. It is eternal. So don't be afraid. Who you really are doesn't remain in your body at the time of transition. Rejoice in the new possibility of leaving behind the body and going forward to a new experience, when the time is right.

*What is the right attitude to our body and to a physical challenge?*

It is just a change in orientation from, "My body is who I am" to, "who I am just uses the body. If who I am is the one that uses the body, I can manipulate this usage as I like. I can compensate in various ways, express myself in different ways. This body was given to me as a gift to use as I wish. If some part is dysfunctional, I will use other parts. This part does not reflect who I am. On the contrary, this provides an opportunity for me to express my wholeness freely, without depending on my body. I identify myself more as the Self, rather than the body."

*How can we help someone who is experiencing a crisis?*

A human being who finds himself in a state of crisis can turn one of two ways: either he can choose depression, a sense of being a victim to the circumstances of life, or he can find new inner resources of strength and hope. He can discover a new channel of self-expression, and use it as an opportunity to grow in a different direction. Any kind of activity derived from strength and hope is a blessing.

A person overshadowed by despair, in a state of panic, has difficulty accepting help. So, your first and most important step is to cultivate in your heart and mind a strong belief in the person's strength, and ability to heal him/herself, and strong hope. You have to find unconditional love in yourself, absolutely free from judgment, and then any help you give will be more powerful.

*Sometimes I feel tremendous gratitude toward my doctors and others who take care of me. How can I ever thank them?*

When you thank your healers, in a way you are thanking yourself, because you are the one who allows the care to take place. You are the one who brings in the healing. You are the one who channels the grace through physicians and healers. You are helping them as much as they help you, by letting the love, the care and the well-being flow through them to you. You are part of this creation. You are not only the receiver, but also the giver. By taking part in this process, you are drawing love energy upon everyone involved. The main understanding here is that there is no separation between you and your healers. You are all one on many levels. There is only one level on which you seem separate, the gross physical level. But beyond the physical body, your bodies are intermingling, your vibrations are dancing together, your love flows together. Your desire to be with Me is one. What could be more unifying than that? Although you are the patient and they are the physicians, you are all different aspects of the same picture. They need you as much as you need them. They need to thank you as much as you thank them. You are all creating together.

*How can we help mentally challenged individuals?*

Love. Only Love will refresh their memory of what they are here for. The more Love, the more memory is produced. They are not here for physical achievements. This is obvious because they were not given the tools in this life for physical achievements. They are here to learn, to coexist under any condition, to love and be loved under any condition, to accept and be accepted, to dance and rejoice, no matter what. They are here to remind themselves of how it used to be when they were all heart. They have an advantage over you because their mind is not in the way. They are here for a lesson. They chose this lesson to reexperience their Heart. This is their main task in this life. They are different for a reason. They are also here to remind you of your Heart. People who can be compassionate toward others are learning just as much as those who give them the opportunity to express their compassion. It is a mutual coexistence for the sake of growth.

September 7, 1996

## 15

## Death as Part of Life

Good morning. In the light of the fear of death, and of the fragility of life; in the light of the misunderstanding of death as part of life, the relationship between them and their coexistence, I would like this to be our topic for today. What are you most afraid of and yet think about and live in its shadow constantly, if not the Angel of Death? You are so afraid of death that your whole life is conditioned by it. Your whole focus of thinking, behaving, living, comes from the desire to be as far away from death as possible. Almost everything you do, consciously or subconsciously, is done somehow with reference to this great unknown--the mystery of death.

Death has relatives--accident, sickness, etc. Some go so far as to consider feelings of loneliness, the fear of being alone, fear of darkness, fear of heights, fear of animals, as a form of death. To suppress this fear, you develop systems upon systems, formulas upon formulas--to separate your life from that unknown territory and its relatives. You develop patterns upon patterns, walls upon walls, on various levels--physical, mental and emotional.

You are living a separated life. You call one 'life' and the other you call 'death.' You like to look at babies; you are afraid to look at old people. You smile and express happiness when you hear good news; you frown, you worry when you hear about someone's disease, someone's death. Your life is conditioned and divided in a very clear-cut way. Where does it lead you? It leads you into finding your own solutions, your own frame of mind, your own understanding of how to maneuver through life in order to avoid this big void. The systems you create for yourself to maneuver around the Angel of Death, to keep him as far away from you as possible, are your efforts to say, "Look, I am not here, just ignore me, I'm not part of this game. Skip me." Based on your limited knowledge and experience in this lifetime, which comes from observing your close surroundings, hearing the news, reading books and so on, you create your own philosophy about how to 'survive.'

The solutions you come up with are very innovative. In fact, they are quite amusing. You take the concept of free will and use it very selectively, saying, "I am a free man, I am a free woman. I can do as I like. I can jog, diet, smoke, eat what I want. I need to take medicine, I avoid medicine. I believe in this or that." But where you really need to exercise your free will is in the big game, not in this little game. You deceive yourselves, thinking that you exercise your free will. Actually, all those little exercises you perform are under the huge canopy that disallows free will. It says, "Life is divided into life and death, and I need to do all I can to avoid death, since death is bad." You see, you lose half the picture.

You think by avoiding death you live; by fighting death, you choose life. Actually all that time you choose to focus on what you fear rather than focusing on what you really want. You deceive yourself thinking that you choose life, but all the time in the back of your mind you have death. You hear people say, "I better not eat the cookie because I already gained too much weight. I'm swimming, it's good for my health. I'm meditating because I want to get enlightened and never come back again. I will kill death before it kills me. I'll save a lot of money so when I get old I won't die hungry, poor and sick." Your orientation and what drives you forwards is your desperate effort to avoid death. This is not free choice; this is a very selective kind of choice. This is living half of all possibilities.

Now, there are two ways to deal with it. One is to advise you to stop, to live for life and ignore death. Pretend death doesn't exist. But this would be a little too ambitious on My side, wouldn't it? You won't take My word for it. You see death hiding behind every corner. You turn on your TV and hear about wars, murders in big cities. Death is all over. You cannot just pretend it doesn't exist, can you? You have heard of miracles, but that's not going to happen to you, is it? The other way is to explain the nature of death, but this is full of obstacles, too. Many people have tried to tell you about the nature of death. You find it quite interesting, but this hasn't really released your fear of death.

Where are the people who choose life, who look at death and see a blessing, an opportunity? Where are the people who see death as part of life, rather than the opposite of life? You can find such people only among those who understand the meaning of Life. They understand that there is something more beyond the nitty-gritty details of life. They understand that beyond the laws of cause and effect there is a higher reality and higher awareness. They understand that who they are is nonlocalized, nonmatter--Vastness Itself, free from the illusion of death.

To use the school system as an analogy, we can say that elementary school gives the basic understanding of cause and effect. You put your hand in the fire, it gets burned. You climb the mountain, you see the valley. You are kind and helpful to people, you receive kindness and help.

A little bit more advanced is the idea that cause and effect operate beyond one's lifetime. Cause and effect operate also in the bigger picture, in the bigger 'connections' of your existence. In these 'connections' your soul chooses a physical embodiment for a specific experience. It learns from this experience and moves forward to another physical embodiment which is based on previous causes. The non-physical soul wishes to experience physical realities, that can be expressed only through thoughts, emotions, sensations and relationships with other physical beings. Yes, there is a connection between lifetimes, even though not on the basis of sin and punishment, as some think. The real understanding here is that, based on the creation and knowledge of one lifetime, the next one progresses in the same direction, not as a punishment, but as the continuation of the course that was set in the previous life. This I would call middle school understanding. When you graduate from middle school, you have a fairly advanced understanding of the game called life, or rather, life and death.

But when you reach high school, your understanding grows. Now you are able to comprehend greater wholeness. Now you can release yourself from the conditions of cause and effect. You can think more in terms of being in the flow. You know that it really doesn't matter so much what you did in the lower grades, what really matters now is to reach the ultimate goal.

What is this goal here in the school of life? The goal is to be free from cause and effect, to rise above fear, above the separation between life and death. The goal is to be only in this one ongoing flow of life, embracing all its parts, everything it includes, since it is all Life. And by accepting it, embracing it and loving it, you melt the fear of death away. Then you understand and experience that it is not you against others, that it is not you living at the expense of others, including the animal kingdom and plant kingdoms. But rather, you together, living life by the grace of each other's existence. You human beings are not here to conquer everything, nor are you here to protect everything else in order to exist. You human beings are here to play together, along with everything else, the play of Life, being part of it, moving forward with it.

It's somehow easy for you to understand the cycle of a tree, a flower, an animal, but it's very hard for you to apply this to your own life. It is the same game. One day cells in your body are so essential that your life depends on them, and the next day they fall off, giving way to new cells, new life. These cycles are infinite.

You are all giving and receiving, giving and receiving. One thing is not more important than another. All of it together flows and moves and changes. Therefore, your goal for high school is the understanding that the Law of change, the Law of ever-growing, is the only Law that exists. With this understanding of the wholeness of life, you realize that in this flowing, you choose to attract to yourself experiences that determine how you move forward. This is where free choice really takes place. Not under a threat, not under a separated understanding, but based on the understanding that physical death is part of this moving forward.

By fearing something, you bring it upon yourself. Cause and effect still exist, but now that your understanding is broader you can choose the cause and thereby change the effect. If you are sick, on some level you chose it for yourself, and on some level you also chose the cause. Nobody did it to you. Remember, you are the main actor in your drama.

If you realize that everything goes somewhere, everything progresses, everything is part of everything else, cycles never end, then you understand that death is part of life. Since an ending is always the beginning of something new, what seems the death of a leaf is just the beginning of new growth. If you choose to include yourself in the world you live in, and if you choose not to exclude yourself from the game of life, you can look at death and not be afraid of it. You can even stop calling it 'death.' You can call it a 'new beginning' or a completion of a cycle. Now you have the deep understanding that nothing really is gone, nothing is finished. Your essence, who you really, is eternal. Rather than look at death as an end, you can feel excited about the new opportunity. Isn't it exciting to begin things?

If you can cultivate this kind of thinking, what you will introduce into your life is the true meaning of free choice. You will release yourself from the huge canopy that hangs over your head that disallows free will. You will release yourself from the major threat to your life. You will truly and honestly be able to focus on Love and Life, rather than on death, competition, hate and the need to control, to overcome, to fight. Then all those things that you were fighting against will dissolve and disappear.

*So will we avoid sickness, not by shielding ourselves from it, but by focusing on health? Will we avoid 'death' not by fearing death but by focusing on life and by including death in life? Is this what you meant?*

Indeed. Riding on the waves of Light and Love is all there is. This is life at its best--eternal Life. The small episode of visiting this time and place is just one station in a glorious journey. Once you truly realize this and take it to heart, you are liberated, free from the illusion of death. Then you are free from the illusion of *any* kind of limitation, because Vastness is the real experience, which, in essence, is beyond experience.

Imagine yourself at the beach, melting into the sand, disappearing between the little grains, but still very much being there. This is who you really are--nonlocalized, nonmatter, no-thing--Vastness itself. Any experience you have that brings you back into a localized existence, any experience, good or bad, is just a station in the journey. It's just something that draws your attention for a while. You see, if you have this understanding, you know that nothing ever ends.

The Vastness is who you are, who you were and who you will be forever. Nowhere is there a space small enough to confine who you are. That includes the body. I know the physical experience of the body in time and space has a strong hold on your awareness. It is a very immediate experience that needs to be taken care of, to receive attention. But within the one-pointedness, within the localized body awareness, there is always an opening, like a flower that opens its petals to the warmth of the sun. Your localized awareness cannot survive without opening to Love and Light, without enabling the Vastness to come in and permeate what is.

I would like you to go beyond, to drop even what seems to you the most progressive understanding, and just be in the Vastness. Ultimately, pure existence doesn't need understanding. Merging with Me is a happening that leaves behind everything that is familiar. It is like melting between the grains of sand in the light of the sun.

*How can I experience more life?*

Life is being immersed in the Breath of God. Life is the awareness of having the grace of God with you, wherever you go and whatever you do. If you let the grace of God shine in you, you have life. When you separate yourself from the grace of God, this is 'death.' You can be walking alive among the 'dead' and you can be 'dead' among the living. Yes, bring God to every action and you will have more Life. Bring light, lightness, love, compassion, joy, expanded awareness to everything you do and you will have more life. Bring your heart to everything you do. See everything first through the eyes of the heart. Open a window in your heart, through which you can look and observe and scan everything around you; then take it to the mind for a final conclusion as to what to do. Then you will have more life.

Life is within you. You have been given the Breath of God. You can let It express Itself or you can ignore It. You can acknowledge God's Breath within you or you can separate yourself from It. Only by choosing the full expression of the Breath of God can you fulfill your desire for more life. Only by recognizing God-within and seeing God in everything and everyone, you will experience Life. From Me to you and from you to Me. I Am you and you are I. From My Heart to your heart and from your heart to My Heart. This is the full expression of Life. And if you can find yourself, in every moment and in every detail and in every doing, within the Breath of

God, every moment and every doing will be a full expression of Life. Then you will experience the real meaning of 'living in the now.'

September 8, 1996
December 10, 1996

## 16

## Love and Politics

Today's topic is love and politics. At first it sounds like a paradox. What does love have to do with politics? But love and politics go hand in hand because they function according to the same Law. They are derived from the same kind of energy, the same mechanism of attraction and non-attraction. Politics is a different name for relationships. Politics deals with relationships between large groups of people. But political qualities can be manifest also in relationships between individuals. In other words, politics is a brand, or flavor, of relationships.

People refer to a political person as someone who puts on a mask and successfully manages to reveal only what he wants to express, rather than express his whole being. In your politics you relate to others only from the mind, calculating the benefits you will draw from the relationship.

*So is politics good or bad?*

"Good or bad" is not really what we want to consider here. What we want to consider is, to what degree do relationships between human beings or large groups of human beings reflect who they are, for the benefit of everyone. How can these relationships create wholeness, harmony, acceptance, coexistence and cocreation in the flow of progress toward a better future? People, individually or as a group, who calculate how to bring about benefits for themselves at the expense of others, use only a fraction of the energy available to them. They ignore the Law of love that encompasses everything everywhere. By choosing to use only a fraction of their being, they disconnect themselves from their own resources.

The Law of love, or what We call the Law of change, the Law of attraction, the Law of oneness, functions in a very simple way. Like attracts like. A politician whose thoughts focus on control, greed and power, attracts to himself people with the same kind of qualities. The chain reaction grows, according to the Law. A politician who thinks thoughts of harmony, ways to bring about peace and a better future, and who honestly represents his voters, surely incorporates both his mind and his heart. A politician with such desires brings wholeness to his individual life and attracts people who strive for wholeness. Together they generate even greater desires to attune with the flow of growth, the flow of energy that created this world in the first place.

A group of people who share the same goals, is more than the sum of its parts. A group of people who truly desire harmony, creates a powerful surge of energy which influences the total environment, and attracts more of the same kind of energy. When such a group reaches a large enough number, it can affect the whole nation to change its priorities in the direction of wholeness. A nation which reflects the wholeness of its individuals becomes a powerful unit. Such a powerful unit, when faced with attempts to divide or control it, can draw on great inner strength to overcome the challenges and become invincible.

Thus, relationships between nations or large groups of people are shaped mainly by the inner qualities of their individuals. These qualities determine whom they elect as their representatives, who are the cream of the crop. In this process of mutual reflection, wholeness is amplified and strengthened. This, in turn, encourages individuals to reflect more of their inner qualities, and to express more of their love, their confidence and their positive view of life and the future.

If, however, the individuals of a group are driven by confusion, separation, anger and desire for control, this will be reflected in the qualities of their representatives, either chosen or forced on them. According to the Law, this kind of relationship between individuals, and between the individuals and their leader, will amplify the desire to separate and control even more--to control nature, other people, other nations. This desire can never be fulfilled because it comes from the seed of separation and lack, and because fulfillment implies wholeness. Wherever wholeness is absent, there is no fulfillment. Unfulfilled desire is a threat to the individual, to the society and to the world. The most important ingredient needed to cure this ailment is Love--the very essence of existence.

A building that lacks a solid foundation, cannot withstand the harsh conditions of time. Your history is full of 'big buildings' that collapsed. When nations managed to keep a sense of shared desire for good, for wholeness, they succeeded. But whenever greed, control and separation took over, they collapsed. The cure for such a situation can be accomplished only at the foundation--at the level of the individuals who make up the nation. Any other attempt, even though well-intentioned, carries within it the seed of separation, which brings the fruit of suspicion and misery.

The only place where a person can find fulfillment is in his own connection to wholeness. A utopian society can be achieved only when each individual is connected to his wholeness, to the Source.

*How can a leader of a country who faces a negative response from a neighboring country use a holistic approach? What are the steps he needs to take to build a bridge toward perfection in the relationship between the countries?*

A great leader must be able to manifest the desires of his people for perfection. A leader is the reflection of his people. Therefore, if they desire courage, power, harmony and love, these are the qualities the leader manifests. In the face of threat, the leader can draw strength from this well of qualities given to him by all his citizens. In the face of threat, a leader who comes from wholeness, who is backed by his society, knows what to do.

When I use the word 'love,' it doesn't mean weakness or softness. Love is energy that can be expressed as power and strength. Only from wholeness do power and strength manifest in their full potentiality. Therefore, if there is a need to destroy, to attack, to take care of business in the face of an immediate threat, a powerful leader, supported by his society, is able to do what is needed. A sick person who needs to take a somewhat poisonous medicine to cure an acute illness in life, doesn't ask, "Is this holistic medicine or not?" He takes the medicine to bring the body into balance where it can regain confidence in its innate ability to function. Only when some balance is restored, a more gentle, holistic way of healing can be introduced to replace the medicine. The same applies to the relationship between nations, between parties or between different sections of government within a country. Deep conviction, that comes from wholeness, has the power to follow through, first to solve the problem, then to bring about balance and restore harmony.

When doubt or opposing desires manifest in a leader, the result is split energy. Then only partial success can be achieved and this invites more opposition. Doubt attracts doubt. The power has to come from wholeness, which is Love. If there is a trace of controlling or overshadowing another group, displaying power for its own sake, it is false power. True power does not bring about opposition, because the impact of wholeness is overwhelmingly uniting. When heart and mind are balanced, the result is goodness and fulfillment for everyone.

*Can you please speak about the ideal society and ideal government? Are there countries which already maintain a state of perfection?*

No, not now. In the very remote past there were small groups, in which, for short periods of time, an ideal society arose. But soon that society turned into a control unit, in which the leaders or the individuals themselves tried to control others in the name of the ideal society.

In an ideal society each member must live an ideal life. In essence, this society doesn't need a political leader. Instead it can use a representative to other societies and before God. The representative is also there to guide the society in a peaceful life style, in coexistence with nature, in coordinating different branches of society, in the exchange of knowledge, etc. A representative of an ideal society is a 'perfected version' of the individuals; they reflect each other's qualities.

*I understand that in an ideal society a leader is an evolved being, who guides the citizens, not by power or control, but by his example of following the highest.*

Yes. You do understand that in an ideal existence, there is no need for politics. Politics is an outcome of a reality that springs from separation. True relationship between two individuals, in which each one sees God within the other, has no room for political qualities. When two nations function in this way and communicate for the benefit of all, they have no need for politicians.

*Are spiritual leaders needed in an ideal society?*

The leaders *are* spiritual. The whole society is spiritual. Spirituality is not a quality that is separate from other activities. Everything is spiritual. Many nations dream about such a future. While the dream is valid and important to keep in mind, attention must be paid to the way religions or groups of people color this vision with their limited realities, concepts and truths.

*What are you hinting at?*

I'm hinting at some people's thinking that there is only one way to bring about an ideal society, thus planting in the desire for wholeness a seed of control and separation.

*You said that a leader needs to represent the people before God. How can he do so?*

Like a high priest. Each citizen keeps God in his heart, and doesn't need a mediator to carry his prayer, his communication, his trust. Nevertheless, there is still an innate desire to find the glory of God on Earth. The glory of God, even though present everywhere, can also be focused in a holy place or a spiritual leader. They can serve as centers for people to come to, to express unity, to express the power of togetherness, to turn to in their communication with God and to amplify the experience of God.

September 9, 1996

# 17

## Nature Is Not Interior Design

Today's topic is nature. I see you are happy about it. Yes, many people on Earth are interested in nature, but many more are not. The latter, who live life detached from the very sustainer of their physical being, look at nature as another 'interior design' in their backyard. But this is not how I would like to begin. I would like to begin by telling you about the glory of nature.

Do you hear the wind outside?
The rain is about to come.
There is order, things come in order.
This cosmic order manifests in everyday life.
The wind is blowing, the rain is coming.
The grass is growing high, grasshoppers are rejoicing,
    people are happy.
The people who work the land are happy,
    they can predict the order.
There is security, there is comfort in the order.
This is the comfort I give you.
You can always count on nature, just as the sun always rises
    in the east and the moon always comes in its time.
I would like to impress upon you that you are a part of it all.
I would like to convey to you, by words and feelings, the
    vastness of nature and how you are an integral part of this
    vastness.
I would like you to sense your strong connection with nature.
Your bodies long for it, they want to attune with nature.
They have the memory of living in the plains and following
    the sun in its journey, following the moon coming and
    going.
They have the memory of living in the mountains, sensing the
    wind blowing, refreshing, giving life.

They have the memory of the oceans, the touch of the
    waters, the talk of the animals.
They have the memory of the whispering of the big animals
    that came from the waters, the joy of the animals that
    once governed this Earth.
Your bodies have the memory of it all.
I would like you to return to nature, once again to walk the
    land and feel part of it, to experience the give and take
    relationship that you once had with nature.
Go to the mountains, set yourself free.
Go to the oceans, talk to the animals.
Go to the plains and swim in the grass.
Dance with My creation, it will bring you so much joy.
Then you will remember how it once was.
It is all in you.
Don't let the mind tell you it is not possible.
It is all possible.
I would like you to go out and feel your minute existence
    and your tremendous existence simultaneously.
Sit on the riverbank and feel lost in the beauty, the vastness,
    the sound, the sight.
Feel like a little pebble that is carried by the water, feel
    insignificant, mortal.
At the same time I would like you to stand on the riverbank,
    spreading your palms to the heavens, roaring your
    mightiness, feeling one with it all, being the river, being
    the pebble, being the sound, being the vastness.
This is the paradox of your existence.


Your immediate impact on nature is limited. Even your grandest
actions make just minute impressions in the ever-changing process of
moving elements, eternally seeking balance and harmony. Nothing
that nature cannot recover from. What does make you powerful? It
is your ability to direct the energy at a very subtle level. It is your
innate ability to synchronize yourself with the eternal movement and

play of the particles that make up nature. Not your bulldozers, your airplanes, your roads, not even your pollution can affect nature to the degree that a single human being who attunes himself to the subtle movement of nature can. This still sounds very complex. Let Me explain.

Your scientists have broken nature down into many categories, subdivided the elements and reached what seem to be the minutest elements--subatomic particles. But all those divided and subdivided elements are still regarded as matter. What is mostly unrecognized or unknown is that you can break it down and continue subdividing it infinitely, and what you will find is not matter at all. What you will find is pure energy--Love.

It is easy to change matter at its subtlest level, where energy becomes matter. The farther you go into concrete manifestation, the harder it is to change that specific manifestation. At the source, before manifestation, matter is comprised of a very specific energy that I call Love. At the source one can manipulate energy most successfully with the greatest results. The flow of Love energy is ever striving for harmony and balance. Only from balance does this flow have the ability to create. The seed-thought of all forms is perfect harmony and balance. But, in the process of becoming more and more materialized, self-created manipulations introduce different intentions, which interfere with balance. This interference, amazingly enough, is self-destructive. It is relative interference in the face of the absolute harmony of creation as a whole.

You, human beings, were created with all your innate abilities, out of Love and perfect balance. Any discord you offer to this perfection makes only a minute impression on the ultimate balance that always exists in the broader perspective. By attuning yourself to Love, to the Source, you can easily create, influence the process of manifestation from non-matter to matter and be powerful beyond imagination.

If you exclude yourself from the attunement to the Source and introduce different intentions, you may be partially successful in your limited reality of time and space, but you will prove to be self-destructive. The huge omniscient striving for balance will smooth out this imperfection, which will return to Totality. However, you can go back to your Origin and become one with the Vastness. Because, You--the aspect of you that is non-matter, the aspect of you that was and is at the source of everything--is the Vastness; is Nature.

*Can you speak about Earth changes?*

Some scientists bring you prophecies of doom, looking at evidence from a limited time/space perspective, but what they see is only a small impression on the vastness of creation. In the face of these doom prophecies you as an individual feel helpless. You indeed feel like the person who sits on the river-bank in awe of the vastness of it all, feeling like a pebble that is swept away by the water. But if you can reach the understanding, belief and experience that you are the pebble *and* the river, then, by bringing yourself into pure thought, by synchronizing yourself with the infinite flow that strives for balance, you can easily prevent the predicted imbalances. You can use the huge, enormous power of the innate striving for harmony, to restore balance. You don't need bulldozers for this. You need only return to the non-matter aspect of you, which is Love, which is Vastness.

Go out to nature, because in your experience of nature in its vastness you'll gain a different perspective than from your limited habitat. You have caged and framed yourself into very fixed patterns of life. You have created so many physical boundaries that, in order to feel free, you first have to break the boundaries to sense the freedom of nature. When you absorb the enormous freedom of nature you can enliven the memory of your own freedom. When you are free you are omniscient, omnipresent. When you are in a state of non-matter consciousness you are master of it all.

If you regard yourself as matter, you are but particles that are swept away in the wind. In this limited state of awareness everything seems more powerful than you. Then you create gods--the stars and the sun, the hurricanes and the earthquakes, the mountains and the ocean, even your concept about what God is--and you feel insignificant. You live your life in slavery, obeying 'masters' that are just matter. But when you find yourself in perfect balance, flowing with creation and nature, you can play all the way in the process of becoming matter, while keeping the perspective of being 'more,' always moved by perfection.

Then you and nature are brothers and sisters. You come from the same place, you go to the same place. You share the joy of Love, carrying within you the Source. Then when you go out to nature, you are not separate from it and it is no longer 'interior design' in your backyard. You are family with nature. Nature laughs with you. You see Light in nature. You see God in nature. There is no room in your heart for controlling or manipulating nature. You live in harmony with nature. Nature lives in harmony with you.

When you synchronize yourself with nature, you will be able to influence nature. You will bring the rain when it is needed. You will stop the earthquakes and other changes that everyone fears. You and nature will cooperate like brothers and sisters, and you will always have perfect weather, perfect conditions, as was originally intended.

Remember how Joshua[*] stopped the sun in the sky so his troops could finish their task? You think that for human beings this is impossible. But remember, you can change nature as long as you flow with it. You can change nature when your pure desire comes from deep within, from You as a creator.

*Can You talk about human beings' relationship with Mother Earth? Who is Mother Earth? Can we increase our support to her?*

---

[*] Joshua (10:12,13)

Mother Earth is the goddess of your Earth. When I say goddess, I mean she is all-prevailing, she is ever there for you. You can't leave her as long as you are alive. Mother Earth provides you with everything, starting from the very early stages of your forming through your last breath on Earth. She is vast, she is omnipresent. Yes, Mother Earth is Me, too. But she has her own existence, just like you do. She is called "Mother" because she provides and gives, no matter what you do. Mother Earth is the substance of which your bodies are made and which sustains you. And at the same time, you are more than Mother Earth, because I give you breath. You are a gift to her just as she is a gift for you. You can worship her, but remember who you are. You can coexist with her, but remember who you are. You can communicate with her, benefit from her, give to her, protect her and be protected by her, but remember who you are. She is the goddess but you are God. You are part of her just as you are part of Me.

October 5, 1995
September 10, 1996

## 18

## Godliness in Everyday Life

There is no one concept of God that is totally shared among believers and non-believers. I don't call them religious and non-religious, because I do not belong in a religion more than outside a religion, as most people think. And this is where trouble begins.

Even though many people accept the premise that God is everywhere and everything, this belief doesn't affect the way they live. Whether or not they call it God, people do have a sense of something that permeates everything. The God they don't believe in is the well-defined God others imposed on them. The well-defined God has different flavors according to different affiliations; and a totally different flavor for the non-affiliated. But whether people believe in God or not, they still keep the concept of God, or not God, in their awareness.

Your reality is made of many associations. Even words like omniscient, omnipresent and omnipotent, used to describe God, have different meanings, depending on the individual's association to these words. One thing is linked to another by memory, by its relative value, by a specific association to a place, a person, a time, etc. Therefore, there is really no abstract knowledge. Every piece of knowledge you gather is connected to a set of previously defined ideas. Even the 'newness' of knowledge is relative to your reality. So the question arises, how do you know that what you have discovered or learned, is the truth? The answer is, that as long as you seek the truth relative to something else, you cannot know. As long as you look for definition, approval or reference, the truth will be relative. When your ideas about what God could be are based mostly on gathered information, rather than on your experience and inner knowing, your truth is relative.

If you desire to have Godliness in your life, or 'be good' as you imagine God to be, if you are a very well intentioned person--you try to apply Godliness in your life according to your understanding. But since this understanding is very conceptualized, you often slip away from your intention. Then you judge yourself for it and promise to be better next time. You even introduce the concept of repentance. Because if there is a concept of some perfect, well-defined way of living and you don't quite see yourself there, it creates a gap in your intellectual understanding. Then you want to bridge this gap, since you are separated from your ideal of what Godliness is.

You can debate the question of God's existence for hours, days and eons, but as long as this is an intellectual exercise, no matter how grand a conclusion you reach, it will still be a relative conclusion, and the experience of separation will prevail. So you can play with the words omniscient, omnipresent, omnipotent. You can keep on saying God is everywhere, but in essence they are just words. God, Godliness, Divinity, Light, Love are beyond definition, are beyond intellectual understanding, beyond your present reality, your dimension, your Earth. God is everything and everywhere, but not your everything and your everywhere.

How do you get out of this loop? How can you accept something, believe in something that is beyond your grasp? That is a question that many generations have grappled with. My answer for you today is: stop, just stop. Don't try and don't fight. What you fight against is really your own internal fight. It's all a game you play with yourself. Just give up this game, this struggle. Stop trying to be good. Stop trying to be bad. Stop trying to be anything. Just be who you are. Accept the wholeness of who you are. Who you are is more than your anger, your desires, your wisdom, your degrees, is more than your job, more than your achievements and failures, more than what other people say about you. It's more than what you think God thinks about you. Who you are is what you accept and allow yourself to be in this moment, and much more. Who you are is Freedom, before all the definitions, before words and before knowledge. Who you are is ultimate choice. If you understand this it will resonate through your whole Being.

At any moment in your life you can choose to express your whole Being, or to express only a part of your Self. To express your whole Being, is to accept God; is to believe in God, is to know God. To express your whole Being is to come from wholeness and absolute freedom--freedom from definitions, freedom from fear, from expectations, from old memories, from anger, from your intellect and from your emotions. Such a place is good, is perfect, because it is not relative to anything. It is flowing, expressed in perfection and self guided. This is Godliness.

*Can you help us understand how Freedom feels?*

Bliss. Freedom from any kind of slavery is invaluable. Look at it this way; if you are anything other than blissful, it's an indication that you are under the influence of feelings, concepts, circumstances, other people's response, stress. You are not free. Try to remember glimpses in your life when you felt free--at the end of a school year, at the end of an exam. Remember how much bliss was created at the end of a war? Freedom is absolute bliss.

*Can even people in prison experience Freedom?*

Yes. This even applies to people whose outside reality is confined, whose outside reality doesn't give them any choices, denies them freedom. It doesn't make any difference, because who you are is not and cannot be confined by others.

*Can we have desires and still be Free?*

It depends on the nature of your desire. Pure desires are a call from deep inside the heart. If you desire wholeness, you are in accord with Freedom. Any desire that is less than wholeness is relative, it confines your Freedom. If you let your mind control your life, you often confuse the desires of the heart with different kind of desires. The more wholeness you experience, the less relative desires will arise. When the inner truth reflects on the outer, your desires are fulfilled spontaneously and you experience Freedom.

*Do we need to bring this quality to our career, to our relationships, etc.?*

Yes. Without being subject to circumstances; without blaming, without judging, without expecting.

*Does it mean that one needs to be above the circumstances of physical life?*

It's you being fully present in all your bodies, dissolving all your boundaries and living the full spectrum of your Being. It's being here and now, everywhere. From this place, you can be above the circumstances.

*As an example, what would You say to a driver, in the rush hour on a busy street, who needs to reach an extremely important meeting? How can he keep his wholeness, his Freedom, if he's late and the traffic is very slow?*

Let go. Stop controlling, stop worrying.

*What do you mean, let go?*

Let go of the part in you that is trying to take over, that believes that by driving faster, by being nervous, by worry, by violence, you will solve the problem. Let go even of the meeting, it's all so relative. It's all but a game, every move is just an option. For every move, there are probably a few more, better moves. Move, do, function, create, but from a larger perspective and higher place. Let this wholeness of yours move you. Imagine you are in a Rolls Royce with a chauffeur. Sit in the back seat and enjoy. Trust that the chauffeur will take you. You are guiding the chauffeur, you are telling him where to go, but you don't worry about the details, the engine, the busy street. You are drinking champagne!

*Let's say, I start on my route to this meeting feeling good. When I begin to feel nervous because I'm late, do I need to let this nervousness express itself, release it and come back to bliss? Is this the way?*

Yes. Not by suppressing, or ignoring the feelings, but by welcoming them and assimilating them into the wholeness. As a good observer, from a high seat, you see everything. You take it all into consideration. You don't ignore parts that might come later and interfere with the wholeness. You deal with them right here and now, make them welcome. Because if you deceive yourself by saying, "Oh, everything will be all right," this is false bliss. Since you are the ruler who sits on a high throne, with a slight movement of your hand, you can orchestrate the whole experience, transmute it into wholeness. Then bliss will grow again.

September 11, 1996

## 19

## The Maze of Life

At this point, let's have an exercise in coming back to wholeness, in finding your way in the maze of life. Although there are surprises waiting at every corner in this maze, the point is to realize that it is all under your control. You have the ability to view the maze from a higher perspective and envision the beginning and the end simultaneously.

When playing with a maze children exhibit various attitudes. One is to look at it and say, "This is too hard, too complicated. I'll start, but I have no idea where I'll end. I might not even find the end." Another child is all excited about the adventure, determined to find the shortest way to the end, and determined to enjoy the process. The child who is enthusiastic about the opportunity to play the game, to explore and solve the maze, goes to the next maze right away, eager for more challenge. Sooner or later, he constructs his own maze, and the game never really ends for him.

A child who assumes it will be too hard, who sees an obstacle at every turn, sometimes makes it to the end but more often gives up in the middle. This approach is so energy-consuming for him, that even if he reaches the end, he will lose enthusiasm for other mazes.

Then there is a third kind of child who begins by anticipating difficulties, but as he overcomes obstacles and does indeed reach the end, he discovers new abilities in himself and acquires enthusiasm on-the-go. There are many thousands of people on Earth now, who came for the sole purpose of rekindling their enthusiasm, remembering how much fun this maze is. They came to rediscover the joy of the game and to create new ones and sweep other people along with their enthusiasm.

As you read these descriptions, where do you find yourself? What kind of a child are you? Do you anticipate an obstacle at every corner, mistrust the process, doubt that you can ever reach a place that will offer new games, new possibilities? Or are you that enthusiastic child who eats challenges for breakfast and lives life exuberantly, with confidence and assurance in the flow, as you anticipate and move toward a magnificent end, knowing that it is just an opening for more games? Or maybe, at this moment, you find yourself among those who are starting to awaken, who are changing their attitudes, shifting from a reality of seeing difficulties, obstacles and hard mazes that need to be conquered, into a new reality of finding enthusiasm in the process, anticipating the next step? Are you a little bit lost in this process, not quite sure how to take the right turns, but at the same time keeping a positive outlook and an innate playfulness that comes with the game?

Wherever you find yourself, know that you placed yourself there. Know that this was *your* choice on a much larger scale. The maze was provided for you, but you wouldn't have received it, if you hadn't asked for it. What is the connection between asking for it, and somehow being presented with it? You are at all times the one who asks for the experience, and the one who provides the experience. You are at all times the whole range of functioning. You are your physical body, your emotional body, your mental body, and your spiritual body. You are also your soul, a soul that belongs to a group of souls, and a group of souls that belongs to the Source. Knowing this connection can change your outlook completely. Knowing that you belong can change the way you begin the maze, the process of discovering the different paths and the way you reach the end. Moreover, this knowing assures you that there are many more mazes where this one came from. So when you are done with this one, the fun is not over. You get to do as many as you want. There is an enormous storehouse of mazes of all sizes and shapes. If you enjoy experiencing one, and you desire more, you'll be provided with more.

What you usually think of as your life is just a beginning of ever-expanding rings that are all Life. You think of life in terms of when you were born, what the major landmarks were, how you live your daily life, your family, your job, your friends, how much money you make, your vacations, the movies you see, books you read, foods you like--that's how you see your life. You sometimes expand a little and include in it your religion and what connects you to other people and places in the world. Then, if you expand your awareness a little more, you know that there are remote, exotic, beautiful places where people live completely differently, and have different cultures. You might even travel there and experience a different kind of life. Now you really feel stretched in your awareness of what life is.

Or, you might explore different turns in your own life. You play with the idea of changing your career, learning new exciting things, maybe even becoming an artist, or collecting rare items. You enter the magnificent world of computers, and think you've discovered a different kind of life. You might even change your mate and feel exuberant with yourself. Now you feel you've already extracted whatever you could from life. What else can life offer you? You've tried it all, you've done it all, you've seen it all.

Well, My friend, there is much more. What you've touched on until now is only the very outermost shell of what life is. So, what seemed to you to be a large and difficult maze in which you skillfully played out all your complex relationships, financial maneuvering, and complicated plans, etc. was just a novice's maze. And while you can pat yourself on the back, you are really just a first grader. There is more to explore.

All I have described so far is an expression of yourself in the physical world, while simultaneously yourSelf expresses Itself in all worlds. In essence, there is no separation between them, the question is, where do you put your focus? How do you perceive the fact that yourSelf functions in all the worlds simultaneously? In what way do you live your life here and now, being connected through your different bodies to the Source? What motivates you when you begin your game?

You see, you are a multidimensional being. If you don't use this multidimensional aspect of yourself, if you choose to express yourself through only one dimension, you are like a person who has a magnificent body but chooses to hop on one leg, believing that the rest of his body doesn't function. Look, there is so much more of you. There are so many more games. Wouldn't you like to play them all? Wouldn't you like to explore, find new possibilities, and experience the joy of more? Or would you rather stay with your familiarities in the physical world, and let the hourglass determine the time for the end of the game? I leave the choice to you.

Now, I've laid out a wider screen for you, and I've made it very clear that you are the one who located yourself where you are. You are the one who can walk farther, turn the corner, overcome the obstacles, and flow happily in the direction you want to go. Now you know that there are no expectations. Nobody waits at the end of the line to give you awards or grades. You are loved for who you are and for where you are. Life exists at every point of your existence. Life is all those possibilities. You don't have to travel anywhere to feel alive. Feeling alive does not depend on different aspects of physicality. Feeling alive does not depend on anything really. Feeling alive is being the seed form of everything, carrying within you the knowing of the vastness of life. How does this apply to your life? A living seed is a person who lives life simply. A person who loves what and where he is, appreciates what he has, while at the same time anticipating with joy the next turn in the maze. A person who knows that life will bring more adventures, that it will lead to an even more magnificent maze.

In your everyday life you can manifest your connectedness to all your bodies and to the Source. You are all of it together in a physical form. You are like a rocket launched from a base. While it travels in space to reach its destination it collects everything it comes in contact with, and brings all these collected impressions, this knowledge, to the point of contact with Earth. But unlike the rocket that ends its journey at that moment, you are just beginning. You are now unfolding and manifesting all the experiences and wisdom you collected. You are now developing into perfection like a beautiful flower.

*Can you talk about the decision making process? Is there an ideal process or method?*

Did you ever play in a maze?

*Yes.*

Do you remember how you tried, and if it didn't work out you retraced your steps and went another way? Was it very painful for you to go back and find another route, or was it part of the game?

*If I was innocent about the whole thing I enjoyed all parts of the game. If I was in competition against another player or against time, sometimes I did it without much enthusiasm.*

You are bringing in a different element, which is your relationship to other beings. There are seemingly two things here. Let's first stay in the arena of you and the maze. When did you find it the easiest and most enjoyable process?

*When I took it lightheartedly, easily, without great expectations, when I just did it for fun.*

And what happened if you didn't find the end right away, and you had to maneuver a little bit?

*I gained curiosity--maybe I'll try it this way or that way. Maybe the enthusiasm became even greater.*

What gave you the strength to keep on going?

*The fun, the joy, having nothing to lose. It was my decision to play and nobody forced me.*

How did you feel when you reached the end?

*Happy, ready to tell my friends. Happy for myself that I did it. Maybe more excited now about doing another one. Or, I did it, I'm happy and it's enough for now.*

What you've just described is how one should live life. You asked how one should make decisions. When you stand in the middle of a maze, you think, "If I go this way, it will take me here, and if I go that way, it will take me there; so I'll go this way, and if it doesn't work I'll come back and go the other way." This is how you make decisions. Simply. The more enthusiasm you have, the less likely you'll have to return. The more joy you have, the less likely you'll 'waste time.'

*Can we use intuition in this process?*

You cannot *not* use it. A child who plays in a maze is entirely present. He is not saying, "Now I'm going to use only what my teacher taught me. Now I'm going to feel what my mother told me it's good to feel." A child uses everything.

*If I have several options, does this mean that I need to pick one, and I don't need to eliminate the others?*

Yes. If it leads you to the end, wonderful, you are happy. And if it caused you some deviation, and this was actually the longer way to where you wanted to go, fine too.

*In a maze there is only one way. In life, can we say there are two or three ways which are OK?*

There are shorter ways and there are longer ways in a maze, too. Now we bring in the other factor. What if you do play a maze against someone else and you absolutely need to find the shortest way because you want to win and you are playing against time.

*Is there such a situation that we play against time, in the real broader perspective? Is there such a situation in life that time is really important other than in our mind?*

No.

*But if I think it's important, what then?*

That's it. Time is your creation. When, as you just described, you play against time, how do you feel then?

*More limited, less joyful.*

Do you feel stressed?

*Maybe not in a maze game, but in the real game of life, yes. If I must be on time at an important meeting, yes.*

So why did you create it for yourself? Why would you choose to create stress for yourself?

*Probably without time society could not function. If people didn't agree on the same reference of time, we could not meet and we could not do anything.*

Whose reference of time? Who said you can't? It's just one turn in the maze. Why does time affect you? Why does it create stress in you?

*Because I feel if I am late for this important meeting, I lose options, I may even lose my job.*

Why do you come up with the assumption that you may lose your job?

*Because I put too much importance on this meeting. Because I'm afraid to lose my job, and then I'll face great challenges.*

In other words, you have decided ahead of time that you may not be able to overcome this obstacle in the maze.

*Because there is a chance that I will be late.*

So, in that moment you stopped being the excited enthusiastic child who enjoys the game.

*So what You're saying is that there are no lost causes.*

No lost causes. As We said, if one way doesn't work, another way works. This obstacle that you anticipated so badly, might turn out to be an advantage.

*If I drive with someone else in the car for the same meeting, and he is dependent on my driving, and I tell him, "It will be OK, relax," he will think that I depend on luck and am not realistic.*

He can stop the car and find another means of transportation. In reality, other people's limitations have no impact on you, unless you adopt those limitation. When you take them on yourself, you become limited. Any pressure regarding time or other people is something you create for yourself. In Reality there is no such pressure. As I said, you are loved and appreciated for who you are and where you are, and nobody awaits you at the end of the line to score you in reference to anything or anyone.

*Is the mistake of this driver who feels he is going to be late and feels stressed, that he gives away his power to his boss, instead of keeping it all and having full control of his life?*

You can describe it that way.

*So there is no situation in which, career, boss or president can control our life?*

Correct. If you understand your essence, which is Freedom. If you understand that you are all of it, you are powerful. There is not even one boss in the world that can limit your Freedom.

*So I just need to realize that I'm here to remain Free. The meeting will happen with or without me and it's OK. I'm Free.*

You are your own boss. You choose the roads. You attract your experiences.

*There are no mistakes? All is well?*

Mistakes exist only in a world of references. The mistake which stems from this world of references is that you empower only one aspect of your being. Experiences that do not come from wholeness, that do not strive to encompass all your aspects are, by definition, partial. Therefore, they are experienced as mistakes, they are experienced as suffering. Suffering indicates a mistake, but 'mistake' is a confusing word. 'Mistake' when it is expressed in your world of association, translates into "I did something wrong. Maybe someone saw me. I should look around, maybe I'll be punished." In other words, you translate the word 'mistake' in relationship to the outside world. And sometimes you even consider God as somebody out there who is going to punish you, too. The mistake I'm talking about is just negligence--neglecting to bring your wholeness into expression.

September 12, 1996

## 20

## Joy and Laughter

Today's message is about joy and laughter--essential ingredients for any journey, for any existence.

The spiritual realm doesn't abide by the law of gravity, whereas matter feels heavy. The word 'gravity' has many connotations: seriousness, heaviness, sadness, failure, anything that pulls you down. No wonder that you call what seems to be the greatest 'failure' of the human race, the Fall. When someone seems unable to function, you call it a breakdown. When someone expresses excess joy or freedom, you tell him to "cool down." In other words, matter suggests gravity, the end of motion, the end of a journey.

Have you ever observed a child flying a kite and the joy she experiences when she orchestrates the kite high above, catching the currents of the wind, running with the kite? Have you noticed how disappointed and sad she feels when the kite falls down, finishing the journey, and is once again motionless on the ground? For many gravity generates familiar feelings and sensations of safety. This sense of safety is false. It creates a life style in which people try to control and hold on to their 'kite,' not letting it fly up above, far away; pulling the strings short. This is true of the relationship between parents and children, of your relationship to money and of the way you relate to animals. This is true of how much new knowledge you are willing to risk acquiring, and still remain on safe ground. This is true of the way you structure your whole life. You hold the string tight for the sake of illusory safety, while paying a high price in the fear-based actions, thoughts and feelings that the heaviness creates. Most of all, you pay a high price in the seriousness with which you perceive yourself and your life. You cannot but be weighed down by the heaviness in your life because it surrounds you wherever you go.

You can sense it more in densely populated areas, in big cities. The seriousness of the structure of the buildings, the traffic, the tight schedules, the way in which everything moves about is so heavy that the whole atmosphere becomes condensed. You realize that the air is polluted in big cities. You can measure chemical pollution but you can't measure the 'pollution' of consciousness. If you had scales to measure the density of the emotional seriousness that envelopes you, the scales would break.

This picture becomes even more serious when the whole social fabric is influenced and weighed down by the heaviness. You find that even children lose their innate joy. Humor is a rare quality in society. Individuals enclose themselves with heaviness, moving like separate units, so that the invisible mantle around them is actually heavier than what is visible in them. This mantle of heaviness adds to the separation you feel from each other, often creating confusion and misunderstandings. It has developed into a distorted invisible sensory system. You interpret the whole spectrum of information that comes to you in the light of the serious attitude with which you perceive yourself. This interpretation creates resistance and fear, and like any other information, this subjective distorted information is stored in your subconscious. It grows over time and supplies you with more data, feelings, emotions and patterns of thought, which flavor each new situation you meet. Then, in the event of a new experience you rely on this distorted information which is stored inside you.

Instead of opening up and absorbing new information objectively, you continue the process of closing in, abiding by the law of gravity that pulls you down into a shrunken, condensed version of yourself. This then takes you farther and farther away from your Source, which is the absolute opposite of matter, which is Freedom--particles bathing in the stream of joy and laughter.

Based on your experiences, you know that joy and laughter are positive influences in your life. But, instead of finding them in yourself, you look for them in entertainment that provides you with some laughter to lighten your day. Laughter has become such a rare product that you have to pay for it. I tell you, your innate structure, your innate quality is joy. It can be expressed in many ways, from the very direct manifestation of laughter, singing and dancing, to a more sophisticated joy expressed in humor, from smiling faces, smiling eyes, to the lightness in which you can conduct your life. Most importantly, joy can be expressed in the lightness in which you perceive yourself. You do take yourself too seriously.

A joyful person is fun to be around, because she produces a rare product, like the fountain of youth, that everyone is after. A joyful person not only radiates her innate happiness, her true nature, but is also free of the heavy mantle of seriousness. Access to such a person is light and easy. She remains open to new impressions, to the natural flow of life. For her the distortion of perceived data is minimal. A joyful person's process of feedback is self-nourishing, since her channels are wide open to receive all the available bubbles of joy that cannot be experienced by others who are clothed in their heavy mantles.

When the sense of lightness is rekindled, it actually affects matter. Scientific research comparing the cells of a very serious person to the cells of a truly joyous person will find completely different structures. The heaviness in a serious person's cells creates higher density that causes the cell to be more fragile, less flexible and less able to deal with outer or inner stressors which cause mutations and distortions. A joyful cell is a loose structure that is more flexible in the face of change. The joy that creates lightness enables the life force to flow from one cell to another, thus maintaining unity in the body. The cells, rather than dealing with challenges individually, rise as a powerful unit, able to achieve wholeness once again.

Joy and laughter are not separate qualities belonging only to jokes or comedies. They are the basic building blocks of the universe. Joy and laughter, like Love and Light, permeate your Life. Joy is the state of awareness from which you all come. It provides you with a new sense of self-worth, of self-definition. It is a definition of non-defined matter. You see, laughter and joy are uncontrollable, endless; they are as expanded as the universe. If they are absent or are not experienced, it is because they were pushed away by fear, worry, seriousness, heaviness, control, and then Life ceases to exist for you.

People's notion about the need to be serious in order to perform a task, is distorted. There is no contradiction between the ability to focus and perform, and the ability to maintain joy. Joy doesn't belong only to the comedy section. Joy belongs to life. You can be the top manager of a high-tech company, run meetings about the most complex, detailed, sophisticated technology, and be joyful at the same time. You can maintain this level of joy in your body while you perform serious tasks. Not only can you; maintaining joy will heighten your ability. It will bring your performance to a much higher peak, and your achievements will be beyond expectations. If every individual in a company experiences joy, the whole place will radiate joy that will affect all communication. New avenues will open, leading to more progress. That is the flow of Life.

The Law of change, of continual progress, doesn't abide by physical laws. Go beyond the law of gravity. Don't let your innate, God-given qualities be blocked and pulled down by heaviness. It is in your hands. You are the one who creates heaviness, and you are the one who can create lightness.

Joy and laughter are very easy elements to like. How can you introduce more of them into your life? Lighten up. Take a big deep breath every once in a while. Smile a big inner smile, checking with yourself that the child in you is still there. You are that child, happy, eager to laugh, eager to play. You are the child of God, born with laughter, eager to live a life of joy.

If your environment clothed you with a heavy mantle while you were still a child by unloading its excess heaviness on you, acknowledge it as a terrible mistake. At the same time, have compassion for the ignorance that created this mistake. Don't hang on to the mistake, the explanations, excuses, blame, judgments and memories. Shake them, shake them off your shoulders. They don't do you any good. They just add to your gravity, they pull you down, condense you, while all you really want is to be a kite. Go back to the original joyful child within you. It's easy. It's in your hands. When you awaken your inner smile and open up, you are nourished with endless joy that will multiply and grow inside you. You will once again be a child of God, as you have always been.

*How can I experience more joy in my life? Should I reframe the way I think?*

Let Me tell you: Joy is already present. Joy is the substance you are made of. It is a basic ingredient that comes long before thoughts, as you know them. The moving 'particles' that characterize energy are joy. Joy is what moves the wheels of everything you are aware of. In other words, it is more than a feeling, it is more than an experience. Whether joy is present or not in any particular experience is utterly dependent on your interpretation of that experience. The seeming absence of joy is derived from false expectations and some veils that were willingly and unwillingly put on, somewhere along your journey. My dear one, joy is available to you. Joy is you, it's time to open your eyes to it. Open your heart, open your door and bliss will come.

> Seek the company of children of all ages.
> Seek the company of wild animals, not by capturing them,
> just by enjoying their playfulness in nature.

Sit on the shore between the water and the sand.
Observe the joy expressed by the waves.
Experience the mutual joy that the beach and the waves give
  each other in a playful dance.
Stare at the night sky.
Observe the smiling stars blinking at you in a joyful dance.
Look at the rays of the sun playing with the clouds.
Feel how light it feels when they come from behind the
  clouds and warm your face.
How you long to have them back when they disappear.
You are of the same essence.
Seek what gives you joy.
Stay away from what pulls you down.
I am the One who 'invented' it all.
Believe Me, life is fun.
It's all a game, play it.
It's all a joyful game.
So lighten your heart and join.

September 13, 1996
December 20, 1996

**21**

## Interplay of Light, Love and Life

Good morning. This is indeed a lovely morning. What makes it different than any other morning? Nothing in particular, except your willingness to welcome it and bless it for what it is. To be free of yesterday, to catch the new trend and surf on it, shedding all the strings that tie you. To look at what is, with a fresh outlook. Your willingness to function from your heart, leaving out any sense of heaviness or attachment that you might have dragged with you overnight. Shed it, just as you shed nightclothes. Put on new attire and know that this beginning will remain vital forever. Look at what is with an open heart. This is the secret behind every success story. This is the secret of youth. This is the secret behind health. This is the secret of life.

There are two fundamental currents that come from the Source-- Love and Light. They originate from the Source and flow with the same purpose--perfection. Imagine two streams emerging from the depth of the sea, having slightly different characteristics, moving toward the shore. They reach the shore at slightly different times and fold back, returning to the depth. Then they return to the shore again and again. They are the currents of Love and Light, that permeate every aspect of creation. They are the expressions of the Silence, and without them nothing would exist in the manifest world.

Light, being energy, comes out and expands and expands. It illumines whatever it touches, wherever it reaches, creating chain reactions of more Light in all directions. You can say that Light is the quality of infinite expansion, growth, and progress. Love comes simultaneously and works on a different frequency, infusing all creation with different qualities: grace, compassion, mercy, desire for wholeness, balance and harmony. So while Light is like a jumping, joyful child, Love adds the touch of a smile and inner strength to creation. Life, the third element, is what enables it all to flow, what smoothes the expansion. Life is the very essence of the desire to exist, to create, to explore and express new realities. The interplay of these three elements in creation is the expressed value of God. All particles, all movements, all species, are created out of Light, Love, and Life

You sense these three currents that flow through you as different attributes of God. You call them 'aspects of God,' giving them various names. But any attempt to isolate the individual currents is futile, because whatever you look at, whether with your bare eyes or under a microscope or through a telescope, or even with your third eye--whatever you look at--will have in it these three currents functioning as one. You cannot isolate one from the other.

Your strength and power are not in your ability to isolate, but rather in your power to use this threefold energy in a focused, concentrated manner and to direct progress according to your desire. You see, the currents are there, and if you fail to see them it is because you come from the false understanding that you can exclude yourself from their Totality. You are part of the enormous Flow that always moves forward. But if you choose to exclude yourself, rather than join, then you are a drop that evaporates in midair, and from the drop's standpoint, the Flow doesn't exist any more.

While these three currents move forward, infusing everything with Light, Love and Life, the Father watches, enjoying the playful progress. Who is this Father? Pre-energy. It is what you sometimes refer to as Nothingness or Silence. But you can't comprehend this Nothingness, this Silence, since you are rolling with the currents. In order for you to have a glimpse of this Nothingness, you have to come back to the Source, where you started your journey.

To simplify, I would like you to know that your existence is like a little drop in the Flow, that moves forward with the currents of Love, Light and Life. But at every moment this drop can return to a state of pre-existence, because it carries within it the seed of its Source. This is a simultaneous existence of yes and no, existence and non-existence. In this context, you are one particle that always abides by the Law. You are carried by these currents, and even if you fail to see your reality in reference to this truth, nevertheless it is the truth.

This is what people sometimes call 'divine plan,' because the Flow is always moving forward from the Source. The three currents never go backward, because they always carry the seed of the Source and include within them past, present, and future. They always carry a seed of the Father. So the yearning to come back Home is always present and very easy to satisfy, very reachable.

If in your life you do not experience progress, if Love is not manifest in your reality, and Light is hard to grasp, it is only because you and the people around you who feel like you, consider yourselves lost drops in the vast stream. The stream keeps on going, it's only you who, for a moment, lose your contact with the Flow. But this is only a moment, because the essence of what evaporated will fall back to the Flow and will keep on going. If, in this moment of forgetfulness, you can find the seed of your Source, the seed you carried with you all the way on this journey, you will draw from this seed all the 'nutrients' you need. You will draw all the energy that will enable you once again to open your eyes to Life, Light and Love, to be once again a joyful particle that joins the Flow.
Am I making sense? Do you have questions?

*Is the Source absolute stillness, without any effect by creation?*

Yes.

*So is the interaction of Light, Love and Life the process of creation?*

It is That. It is all there Is.

*Are they the essential qualities of the Absolute? Of the Creator?*

They are the qualities of All There Is, in action, in motion.

September 14, 1996

## 22

## Perfect Social Interaction

A new week begins.
A new opportunity to focus on the now.
A new opportunity to stay in the now forever.
Stay with Me.
Stay with Me in love and compassion.
Stay with Me in joy.
Stay with Me in action.
Stay with Me, focused on the Light,
focused on the Knowledge, carried by trust.
The rest will fall into place.

Any social interaction is a reflection of one's needs and desires. As a reflection it doesn't really have a quality of its own except tranquillity itself. Imagine a lake, a body of clear water, reflecting its surroundings. The effect, the beauty that is created is doubled. The world seems complete. Perfection reflects perfection. Now throw a stone into the lake. A new element is added. The tranquillity is disturbed.

How is this like your social interactions? Two human beings who come together in wholeness and clarity bring greater wholeness. A few people who come together in wholeness and love bring even greater wholeness. The power and beauty of a large assembly that gathers for the sake of love, worship, creativity, progress, focused on the now for the good of everyone--the power of such a group is enormous. Each member provides pure reflection for the others. The members of such a group feel empowered, enthusiastic. They are ready to go beyond, because the trust that's created, as a result of the positive energy, allows full expression of each member's wholeness. This is an ideal society.

Social interactions, as you often experience them, introduce ripples in this perfection. Human beings coming together with less than perfect motives--for personal gain, or to reveal their own imperfection in the hope of finding support--create a wavy, turbulent lake. This is expressed and felt on both the personal and group levels. It creates situations where the energy that is summoned is partial, therefore progress is partial, or there is no progress at all.

What is the cure for this 'disease?' How can you make sure that nobody throws a stone into the lake? When you witness the ripples, what do you learn from this in order to restore perfection? First, it takes a desire for perfection, a recognition that what is, could be better. It requires the willingness of each member to first reflect on himself, and find the cause of the ripples. As I said before, social interactions provide a reflection of one's needs and desires. What are your needs, your desires and goals when you come together with a group? Do you contribute to the ripples? Or do you offer perfection?

Obviously, you as social beings have the need to come together, some less, some more, but you all need interactions that help you to reflect your own being. This is the way you grow toward oneness, and express the qualities of oneness. This is also where you deviate from oneness. It is a three-in-one relationship: between you, your counterpart and God. The question is how you reach balance between these three to create one. You cannot create this three-cornered unity without offering your own perfection, no matter how much you want others to be perfect. Therefore, you have no other direction to look but into yourself. Sometimes you come into an interaction carelessly, but since the interaction will reflect yourself to you, you will immediately recognize your own imperfection. Then, you have the choice to remain in this imperfection, or to strive for a change.

How do you create ideal social interaction? First by identifying either what you lack or what you love in yourself. Both are very good catalysts for social interaction. You lack something, you can attain it by observing it in another--fine. You love something in yourself, you go out to experience more of it--fine. As long as this coming together creates a greater wholeness--fine. Are you happier? Are you feeling enthusiastic? Are you experiencing love, joy, tranquillity, perfect reflection, no ripples? If so, wholeness has been achieved.

If you feel disappointed and have a sense of lack, if you detect feelings of competition, envy, a desire to be more than others, and to see them as less than you; if you feel that the coming together doesn't lead anywhere; if you feel many ripples are created, then ask yourself whether your desires and needs were fulfilled. If you find they were not, check your desires. If they were fulfilled, and still you have the same feelings, then again check the quality of your desires and needs. There is no point in asking these questions of other people in the group. You have no business finding out about their desires and their needs, until you are clear about your own desires and needs, your own reflection. Are you the one who throws stones or the one who offers tranquillity? Only when you are clear about these questions, can you reevaluate your social interactions.

If you find that you desire to continue the interaction, in spite of lack of fulfillment, ask yourself why. "How will I be different this time to achieve greater perfection?" If you find yourself wanting to leave the interaction, again ask why. If you leave with feelings of blame, guilt, anger, you know that *you* didn't allow the creation of the perfect triangle. You were the missing link. The only possibility of creating this threefold, whole relationship is by you being absolutely present and offering perfection.

For a society to move forward in creativity, enthusiasm and achievements and maintain mutual caring and love, the members need to create numerous threefold interactions. Any two individuals coming together in wholeness, automatically bring in the third angle, God, for a perfect structure. The triangle can be expressed in many ways. You and your mate, your classmates, your study group, your work group, your sport group--you, in every interaction in your life. It all stems from you.

In the process of parting from structures to create new structures, a tremendous learning opportunity is offered. New possibilities open to create new structures, greater perfection, greater wholeness. If, from time to time, you have a feeling, or thought, "I don't need anyone, I can manage by myself," you soon find that this doesn't abide by the Law. By the Law of change, your desire for greater perfection will attract perfection. While you continue forward you will find your way to wholeness, you will find new social structures with greater perfection. There is no other way. The structure can be completed in multiple variations. It doesn't have to be in a physical form. Perfection abounds.

*Is it OK to discontinue a social relationship and move on?*

Everything is OK. The questions you want to ask yourself are: "Why, and with what kind of wholeness do I move on?"

*If I feel that a meeting won't bring me joy, or I just don't have it on my priority list, is it OK to avoid such a meeting?*

You didn't quite ask yourself 'why.' The 'why' is not a light question. It's a very deep question. What are you trying to avoid by not being in the meeting?

*If the answer is that there are all kinds of social rules, and I just feel it's not the place I want to be, it doesn't bring me any progress in the direction I want, is it a good enough reason ?*

It is a good enough reason only after you have probed deeply 'why?' and found yourself in a place of wholeness. If, at the end of the probing, you have guilt, or you feel that you are judging other people in the group for not doing what you like, or for being what they are--any of these kinds of feelings mean that you are not leaving with wholeness. You want to make sure that in your triangle you offer wholeness. Only if you are sure that you offer wholeness, are you ready to move on to greater wholeness. But if you leave it unfinished, unclear about your role, nothing is achieved, you are not ready to move on to greater wholeness. You'll try the same structure again and again, until you learn to leave it with wholeness. Thus you find people marrying the same kind of person again and again, you find people trying the same kind of jobs again and again, or the same kind of interactions, and they leave blaming others.

*If during a meeting I have a need to judge, what is the best course of action? Is it best to react or to remain silent?*

Find your place of wholeness. First, always find your place of wholeness, before any reaction. Whatever comes from wholeness will be perfect.

*Thank You very much.*

Indeed.

September 16, 1996

## 23

## Parents as a Model of God

The Fifth Commandment speaks about honoring your father and mother so that your days may be lengthened. The first five commandments are mainly a proclamation of God's Oneness, and the next five are about human beings' choices in the light of their recognition of God's Oneness. So why does honoring parents belong to the first five? Because parents are the model of God on Earth, representing God's male and female aspects in perfect balance. Parents represent God's power of creation, God's unconditional love, God's infinite knowledge, God's quality of giving, God's quality of inspiring, of being ever-present. In other words, parents are God's messengers, whether they are aware of it or not.

Everywhere on Earth parents are there for the newborn from the very first day. In every culture, in every society, there is an inherent understanding that parents are the sole providers and caretakers of their children. And while their deeper understanding of the child's nature varies from one family unit, or society, to another, the basic physical nature of this relationship is shared by all. Like God, parents provide the child with food, with shelter, with warmth and comfort. They are always present for the child.

Each relationship between parents and child creates a three-in-one unity. Even if there is more than one child in the family, the three-in-one unity is still kept between the parents and the child. This three-in-one unity provides the basis for the child's development and acknowledges his growth into his mental, emotional, and spiritual bodies. In cases of a single parent the three-in-one unit is kept, even though it is not obvious, because the single parent takes upon himself or herself the missing aspect. Naturally, a parent who comes from wholeness summons both masculine and feminine energies. If one parent is missing, while in nonphysical or physical form, the other compensates by calling upon the needed energy to maintain the triangle. The spiritual help given to this parent is tremendous, because of the need for the triangle to exist.

The three-in-one structure is essential for the child's smooth development into a being who maintains easy flow between the physical, mental, emotional and spiritual bodies. This structure is the child's ultimate connection with the Vastness--with that aspect of the Being that is free of all bodies. This sense of Vastness is instilled in a child mainly by his parents. Only by the threefold relationship between parents and child can knowingness of God be established smoothly. While parents caring for their child is innate, the child's bond with the parents is a matter of conscious or unconscious choice. Since it is a matter of choice, you are commanded to honor your parents.

You are reminded that the three-in-one structure is absolutely necessary for Life, not just your present physical life, but eternal Life. Even when you are grown up and physically, mentally, emotionally and spiritually independent from your parents, the bond that was created still exists, and must be maintained forever. The bond goes beyond this lifetime, into different lifetimes, different journeys.

There is a common vision, a common purpose that is fulfilled in different varieties of three-in-one relationships, in different journeys, different lifetimes. Honoring parents refers to both the immediate physical life and to other forms of life. A strong three-in-one connection of three souls--father, mother and child--holds within it the very essence of God. This is the ideal form to bring one to the realization of God.

Unfortunately, there are many factors that interfere. The most obvious one is the misunderstanding of this holy structure, which results in its misuse for lower purposes. When, in a relationship of parents and child, elements such as anger, control, attachment, physical or emotional abuse or conditional love interfere, the holy structure cracks. The basic vehicle, the chariot that leads one to God, is damaged, slowed down. In a triangle each side reflects the others. If discord is offered on one side, it is immediately reflected on the other two sides, thus creating greater disharmony. While the physical body continues to exist, the effects on the emotional, mental and spiritual bodies is amplified to an even greater extent. Thus you may see complete, beautiful physical family structures, but find cracks on the emotional and mental levels which leave deep traces on the spiritual level, offering discord to the journey of everlasting Life, to the realization of God.

As I said before, your physical body and your physical relationships are just tools that help you build other structures. Imagine an upside down pyramid in which your physical body is the layer at the bottom. This physical layer is the foundation on which you build your emotional and your mental layers. They in turn are a very important foundation for a glorious spiritual layer. This four-layered structure is a base for infinite possibilities, for becoming an eternal structure that's always established in God, to expand into more and more glorious structures. In order to maintain this upside down pyramid, with the physical being the lowest layer and then expanding to infinity, qualities of wholeness need to permeate this structure. Parents and child as a unit need to bring to the structure qualities of the Source. These qualities are like cement that holds together and permeates all the layers in the structure.

"Parents as a model of God" is another way of saying that man was created in the image and likeness of God. Enlightened parenthood establishes a three-in-one relationship which is wholly holy. This kind of parenthood exists only for the sake of God, for the sake of Oneness, love and progress. It does not introduce actions, emotions, or thoughts that are not in accord with God. If from time to time one forgets his or her vast existence, and focuses on the limited reality, losing the bigger picture, then the only way to correct it is by coming back to wholeness. Any attempt to deal with the deviation by focusing on it, just creates a bigger crack in the structure. Quietly acknowledge the deviation, and come back to the path, to wholeness. You don't need to explain anything to anyone. Even if you choose to apologize, this is only an external action. Your own coming back into wholeness is what will make the difference at any moment, no matter how big or how old the crack is. Your commitment is to this threefold structure and the commitment never leaves you, even if one or two members of the structure are far away or not in physical form any more.

At any time one can restore the structure by acknowledging the mistake, introducing love, and desiring to come back to wholeness. In this return much joy is produced, self-generating joy and love. The same innate joy and love that were there in the moment of creating the newborn child, can be restored at any moment, no matter how deep the cracks are. If one has this deep spiritual understanding, and a desire for spiritual growth and unity with God, one can appreciate the importance of the fifth commandment, and strive to restore and maintain balance to this three-in-one relationship.

Heaven and Earth are connected at all times. There is a two-way mutual interaction between actions which come from human thoughts and manifestations which come from the Source. Both reflect and influence each other. What you do, what you say, what you think, what you feel, not only influences your own path, it influences the journey of your close three-in-one structures--your parents and your children, as well as larger and larger structures. All your social relationships influence your relationships on the soul level and vice versa. Moreover, these structures continue to expand, and in turn they influence every aspect of your creation, your universe, and other universes as well.

Your striving for perfection has to begin with yourself. When you have this understanding, you can easily apply it in any relationship. At first, it is a conscious activity, but then gradually perfection will spontaneously reflect on all your actions, your thoughts, your interactions. At any moment in your life, you are either a son or a daughter, a mother or father, a friend, a teacher, an employee or employer, a leader or follower--at any moment in your life, what happens in your relationship with others is based first on your relationship to yourself and your relationship with God.

The simple action of turning your face to Me, the simple recognition that God is here and now, can bring a revolution not only to your own being, but also to the whole world through your immediate relationships. If this message is clear, We have accomplished Our mission.

*What is the ideal reason for having a child? Can you talk about family planning?*

Planning is exercising your freedom of choice in navigating your physical life. What is decreed spiritually will happen anyway. If spiritually there was an intention to bring forth the third element in the three-in-one structure into physical embodiment, this will happen. Whether it comes in love or not is a matter of choice. The more love you flow into the channels of creation, the smoother the journey will be for the newborn, and the greater the chances for spiritual growth.

*Can you talk about the ideal preparation a couple can make prior to having a child, preparation on the physical and the spiritual levels?*

Since the creation of the child prepares a physical palace for the soul, like a very good king, you would prefer to use the best materials to build this palace. You might even consult the stars as to when it would be good to have this palace built. You might consult with the musicians about the perfect music that should be sounded in the different rooms of the palace. You might consult the gardeners about the beautiful gardens that surround the palace, etc. Parents who are consciously preparing for their creation can use all their knowledge and skills to build this magnificent palace. It could mean different things in different cultures. The intentions put into this preparation will generate more and more love, which is the main ingredient necessary for the process of birth and growth of the new baby.

*So it's not only the planning to start the process of having the baby, and not only the preparation for the physical uniting of the parents, but it's a preparation much before that--in their physiologies, their intentions, before the physical coming together.*

The couple planning a baby should always strive to maintain wholeness. Any doubt, stress or discomfort introduced in the process prior to intercourse will lay an unwanted foundation for the new creation. But no matter what precedes the intercourse, physically, mentally or emotionally, the magical moment of mother and father creating a child, a new three-in-one structure, is a new beginning, is holy. It's a here and now experience.

*Parents sometime have a desire about the sex of the child or qualities such as a musical talent or a physical trait. Is having such expectations desirable? Can parents attract a specific soul, a specific child to their experience?*

They can, but this attraction happens mainly on the soul level. Nevertheless, desires that come from the physical embodiment of a soul, can alter soul-based decisions, if they come from wholeness and love for the highest good, if they offer a strong three-in-one structure that brings the experience of unity.

A child is born with innate qualities, purposes and possibilities of expression. When given Godly support, free of stress and control, he or she will naturally unfold what he or she came to experience. The parents can sustain, support, be there in times of doubt but they cannot make choices for the child, just as God doesn't make choices for you.

September 17, 1996

## 24

## Is Darkness Real?

The concept of light and darkness lies at the very essence of your existence. You move through the universes by the power of Light, but still you assume that darkness chases at your heels. You sense, you hear, you see the power of darkness in action, and as you experience it, you turn it into an essential part of your reality. You see it, therefore you believe it exists. You experience it, therefore it is real. "There is no doubt about it," you say. "Everyone sees it."

What is that force that you find yourself dragged into, that is not the Light? Why do you experience it? Why is it there? And why, for God's sake, did God create darkness? These are some of the most fundamental questions people have asked through the ages.

You are, in your very essence, a seed that comes from the void, from Nothingness. In this Nothingness, complete stillness, that is nonqualified, nonquantified, nonexpressed, your essence has a desire to become seen, expressed, understood, experienced. This desire introduces polarities in the awareness that lead to an action: from nothing to something, from stillness to activity, from void to existence, from no-light to light. So, in the very early stage of creation, polarities are introduced.

In essence, everything you see, hear and experience as your manifest reality has polarity inherent in it. This is what creates progress. Every manifestation begins in Nothingness. A desire for something arises, polarity is created, and then the process of creation that bridges the poles takes place, until wholeness is reached. From wholeness the process begins again and again. Wholeness itself is balance, without desire. But from wholeness new desires arise and the cycle goes on and on. This stands at the essence of your creation, of everything that constitutes your reality.

Now, what is the energy that helps this process? What helps to bridge the polarities, to create something out of nothing, and to reach wholeness again and again? It is the energy of Light. Light flows together with Love, they are the essence of Life--the eternal flowing of the process of creation. By simple logic, if Light, Love and Life are the very energies that enable progress, any opposition to these energies will slow down progress, will slow down the bridging of the polarities.

A process of creation that bridges polarities by the energy of Light and Love enjoys full expression to glorious heights, to perfection, until it reaches wholeness again. A process that chooses to ride on energies that are in opposition to Light and Love, finds itself in an eternal state of polarity. The bridging is impossible. Beings who indulge in this kind of self-expression might find great satisfaction in the fact that they do express their desire. They live in the illusion that they reach moments of glory, since they have never experienced their real glory. You see, glory that comes from self-glorification, just to manifest a desire, cannot last, because it doesn't have the energy to reach wholeness again. It is like a bridge that never makes it to the other side.

Still, during those moments of self-glorification and satisfaction, a memory is created and registered. All creation witnesses, registers and accumulates these moments of brief success of the power that uses darkness as its vehicle, thus creating an entire hologram of a reality that expresses darkness. The evidence of momentary successes of the darkness that has been accumulated for eons and eons and the impressions that were imprinted on the memory bank of all beings are enormous. So even if one chooses to ride the wave of Light and Love, these impressions chase at one's heels, always demanding attention, always offering an alternative wave to ride.

Even though in the beginning, Light and Love seemed to be the only vehicle or option, now, for many beings, darkness and Light are two equal options. As a matter of fact, you experience both options almost every day of your life. The accumulated memory of a vast range of experiences, your personal experiences and those of many others, has an enormous effect on you. I would say, most of your subconscious is fed with negative experiences. Since your subconscious plays an important role in the way you function in daily life, it convinces you time and again that darkness and Light are two equal powers. For you, darkness is a substantial reality, has power that you cannot overcome, and prevails, no matter what you do. The fact that you see evidence of it wherever you go continues to strengthen this illusion. For many people it becomes the only reality. What's left then is only a vague idea of something which you call hope. You often use the word hope as a vague possibility for an escape from your dark reality. If you hold on tight to this hope, you believe you will find a way out, and indeed you sometimes do.

But there is an entirely different way to consider the situation. Since you are always the seed *and* its manifestation, the source *and* its expression, you can rise above this hologram. You can rise above the all-too-convincing manifest reality that's all around you, which you believe threatens to swallow you. You must go back to that initial state of your being, where you chose the Light and knew only the Light, where none of the accumulated memory had a hold on your subconscious, where you were pure and all of your being was Light and Love. From this place you can get rid of the hologram that seems so real and start anew. You can ride the energies of Love, Light and Life, bridging the polarities to reach wholeness.

The power of darkness and all its manifestations is not only imprinted on the screen of your subconscious, but is also very evident in your conscious state wherever you go. How can you erase the seemingly huge quantity of accumulated data about this power? Where do you get the strength, the vision, the imagination, even the desire to say to the darkness, "You don't really exist. You are just an illusion."? How do you deal with this when it comes right at you, demanding attention, imposing itself on your reality?

What often seems impossible on the level of action, can be achieved by a slight shift of awareness, that requires no effort, toward a different existence. You must dare to believe that there is a different reality. This daring is more than just a hope, even more than a tremendous amount of action to fight the darkness. I am talking about inviting the forces of Light and Love to take their place, side by side at first with the darkness, then trusting and believing in their power until they illumine your whole reality. Then you are fully in the Light. This can be done in a few minutes in the confines of your individual existence, wherever you may be. Or, it may take the effort of a number of human beings who share the same desire to maintain the inner flame of Light and nourish it until it grows enough to take hold of their reality. Or, it may take ages.

For Light to bring wholeness, enough original memory needs to be introduced, enough beings need to have a strong desire for the Light. More and more beings need to see Light as the only possible way to eliminate darkness from their reality. Darkness has power only because human beings hold it in their minds and their memories, help it grow and believe in its power. Many of you do it very innocently. Each time you say, 'touch wood,' you acknowledge the power of darkness. It is as innocent as that.

Remember, darkness is part of your reality only if you allow it to take hold of your reality. The more you believe and choose to be in the Light, the less and less darkness you will see or experience. So it is not just a matter of hope. It is a matter of daring. It's a matter of a conscious choice you have to make, just as you did in your essence at the beginning of time. You have to choose to ride the energy waves of Love and Light. You have to reclaim control over your reality rather than being swept away by it. The stronger your faith in the power of Light, the less you will need to hope and the less you will see darkness. Know that at every moment you can reclaim your power. At every moment you can choose to have an entirely different view of your reality, and create a new reality. Being established in the reality that says, "faith, light, love, strength and power," enables you to go out and deal with what is. What is out there will continue to knock on your door, but you will have the choice to lock your door to the darkness or transmute it.

What I am telling you here today is not just a theory. It is your only option, because if you let the darkness take over your reality, you become partners with darkness. But no matter how powerful darkness is, it cannot erase the original memory of Light. It cannot achieve its goal. It is self-destructive. If you choose to be part of this destruction, know that this is a momentary experience. Once you go back to your seed form, you are always at the beginning of a new journey, where you can choose Light again and again. You need to keep on trying again and again, until you learn to see Light and Love as your only options, until you recognize that you are Light and Love, until you never allow darkness to take hold of you. At that glorious time, you will be victorious, because you will once again experience wholeness and perfection.

September 18, 1996

## 25

## The Multidimensional Journey

Michael,* Michael all is well.
The purity of your heart is shining forth golden rays of
    warmth.
Your gentleness and softness are like sweet music to the ears,
    like a warm bed for a baby.
You are a beloved child of your Father and Mother creating
    wholeness wherever you go.
Come, Michael, let's walk together the path of life spreading
    seeds of joy for others to reap.
Come, Michael, let's climb together the steep mountains of
    glory for the joy of viewing the golden fields of love.
Come, Michael, let's fly together and visit all of our children
    who open their petals to us.
Let's drink from their nectar and leave our blessings wherever
    we go.
Come, Michael, let's join hands for life.
Let's join hands for eternity because our spirits have been
    roaming the land since the beginning of time seeking to
    beautify and harmonize, to bring back lost children .
We welcome you amongst us, our brother.
Come, let's join the journey forever more.

Our love is extended to you ones for the purity of your hearts.

*Who are you? Can you tell us more about yourselves?*

We are the Angels of Peace. Messengers of the Most High to
support you on your way.

---

* *Dear reader, you may insert your own name instead of Michael (and 'sister', as needed)
and enjoy the invitation.*

Your world as you have come to understand it, is expanding as your awareness expands. As you open to different possibilities, your reality expands. One aspect of your reality centers around your well-being, your surroundings, your needs and your development. Parallel to this, you keep a corner in your mind for the possibility of other lives outside of Earth. Information about life on other planets, UFOs, mysterious visitors, different beings, is everywhere. For most it is kept in the background, as a parallel possibility. For a few, it becomes a central focus in their lives. But even though the reality that includes parallel lives has dawned on you and you are gradually willing to accept it, you still view it from a very physical and conceptualized point of view.

Since you understand life to exist only in a certain set of variables--biological, chemical, etc., you look for signs of other life in terms of this set of variables. You are looking for physical evidence to fit your concept of life. If you find pictures of UFO's you see it as the ultimate proof of a different existence. This is due to your partial use of your own being, and your belief that only what you see, feel, and think exists. You are oblivious to the fact that there are other existences, and that there is more of you.

When you broaden your concepts and allow the expansion of awareness in your own being, you find that the reality around you expands and grows as well. The more you accept the depth of who you are, the more you discover your own abilities. The more you are willing to connect through your heart with your Source, the more you will be able to experience other existences.

Presently, you experience your dimension mainly through your physical, emotional and mental bodies, but when you expand and open up to include your spiritual body, more of your being, then you will simultaneously experience more dimensions. Your inner awareness is reflected in your outer awareness. Therefore, when expansion of awareness takes place, you open the door to a process which stretches your concepts. Then, you will begin to require less physical evidence for things to be included in your reality. And the less you require physical evidence, the more your awareness will continue to expand and experience many dimensions.

You already know about people who bring you evidence from other dimensions. Even the book you are reading right now requires a great amount of stretching and you can't help but ask yourself what's real and what's not, whom you can believe and whom you cannot. To resolve this question, you are again looking for evidence. But know that inner journeys, in contrast to outer journeys, are more subjective, in the sense that you cannot bring physical proof for them. Therefore, what can become your own truth is not necessarily your neighbor's truth.

Different people experience different rates of expansion, different rhythms of opening to other dimensions. I do not want to put the rate of expansion in a hierarchy, so as not to create expectations or disappointments. A person who is curious enough will find all the answers on the way, enjoying the surprise of the exploration. The purer this exploration and the more innocent, the more help will be given--physically, through books, friends, etc., and non-physically, by the elements of the explored dimensions. Therefore, my dear ones, don't try to impose any order on the vast information that you find. Know that as many spiritual journeys as people make, that's how many pieces of information will be hinted at or revealed.

The most important and valuable learning experience in this journey is opening to the understanding of many dimensions, the understanding that the outer journey coexists with the inner journey. It might seem to you that there is a paradox--the deeper you explore in your inner journey, striving to be who you are, the more you get the sense of Vastness--you being a creator. And the wider you go in your exploration of other dimensions, possibilities and experiences, the more you realize how minute you are in the midst of all possibilities.

This is a paradox that many of you find hard to bridge, but it is a very blessed paradox, because it stimulates expansion. In essence, this is the process of creation, the desire to know more, to explore, to go where nobody has gone before. The way to integrate the paradox is to ride on the energies that take you out and take you in, that expand and focus. These energies that assist your exploration are, in essence, one and the same energy, no matter in which direction they are aimed. Even though it will seem to you that you run in parallel lines, you are running to infinity, where all lines meet; where the macro and the micro, the broad and the focused, the expansion and the contraction--all meet in unity.

The energy I want you to join whole-heartedly, is the energy of creation, which is Light. By becoming a pure particle of Light, you join the current and you become the Light. The journey that you all participate in is a multidimensional journey. The decisions and choices you make, the thoughts you produce, the feelings you radiate form your dimension and determine your relationship to other dimensions. Even though you sometimes see yourself as a very small particle, with a minute ability to make a difference in the vastness of the universe, the choices you make do determine whether you will be a particle of Light who joins the stream, or not. By becoming a unit of Light you become a unity of Light.

To help you resolve this paradox, let me come from a totally different angle, and give you some advice. My advice has to do with the way you go about your life. Keep a door open. Don't lock all your drawers and closets, don't conceptualize everything. Leave all your conclusions somewhat open. No matter how scientific you are, how concrete and busy your life is, or how deep you feel sunken in the heaviness of life, leave the door open. Because it is your own inner journey that will determine your outer journey. There is nothing to be afraid of, nothing to lose. God is here and now for you.

September 19, 1996

## 26

## Cut Your Strings of Attachment

The word 'string' hints at some connection that pulls you, attaches you, gives control to something other than you. Attachment is the opposite of Freedom. Freedom is the state of the Absolute. Only the Absolute is pure Freedom, and only creation that reflects the Absolute can express Freedom. When God created the human soul and breathed the breath of life into human beings, that creation was infused with the creative powers of God, which are Light, Love and Life. That creation is in the likeness of God, a pure reflection of God. It is in a state of absolute Freedom, and always maintains the Presence of God in seed form.

But Freedom diminishes when imperfection is introduced into creation. The human soul in its desire to create, puts on 'garments' that choose to express themselves. In the process of this ongoing creation, these garments express desires which do not necessarily reflect the Source. They, in turn, put on more garments that produce more desires that introduce more qualities that don't reflect the Source. The farther away the various manifestations move and the more they accumulate imperfections, attachments--the less free the human soul becomes.

A soul in its pure state is pure bliss, is Light itself. But when the soul begins to put on garments upon garments, the pure state of bliss is covered with increasingly denser qualities. The thicker the garments become, the more strings of attachment there are, the less Freedom is experienced. The physical embodiment in the three-dimensional human form, could be considered the outermost garment of the soul. It is the most condensed form of Light, which experiences less Freedom and more attachment than any other manifestation on the soul's journey.

Most people, being foreign to the experience of Freedom, are disconnected from the pure seed of Light inside them. They look at their life only in relation to the outer garment. They define, discriminate and judge life only in reference to the three-dimensional world they live in, rather than viewing their life in reference to the whole, to the pure absolute freedom that rests inside them.

In its broadest definition, attachment is everything in your life that is not in the Light. Attachment is everything that doesn't abide by the Law of change, the Law of love, the Law of progress, the Law of oneness. Anything in your life that does not give you an experience of flowing joyously in the stream of Light--be it a thought, feeling, action, relationship, belief, concept, habit, attitude or mood--is an attachment and pulls you down.

But as you can clearly see, these experiences are totally subjective, they are all, on some level, your choices, and do not now and will never include anything imposed on you from outside. 'Freedom,' a word that is very widely used in your language and history, is mistakenly considered as something received from others, or held back from you by others. In reality, Freedom is the quality of Light. Freedom is the essence of creation, the essence of your soul. Freedom is who you are. Therefore, nobody can take it away from you.

Any experience you have that is less than Freedom is one that you alone created for yourself on your journey while accumulating garments, and clothing your soul with them. You set your own limitations by putting your attention on the limitations, on what is not rather than on what is. Wholeness encompasses everything, it is omnipresent. And any experience which is not perfection happens because you introduce little black spots on the surface of this wonderful ball of Light that is You. Nobody can put black spots on the ball of light and nobody can take them away unless you allow it to happen. This is your dominion and you can initiate anything you want at any time. All you need is the conviction that you can take charge, and that it is simple. How? By reconnecting with the seed of Perfection that lies within you.

If you do find it hard to cut the strings of attachment that prevent you from moving forward into the Light, you can ask for help. But help can be given to you successfully only if you allow the change to take place. Only if you truly desire to be in the Light, only if you truly want to let go of the strings, can you look at the seed of Perfection and say:

I am Your pure reflection.
Who I am is Light, and I don't want anything less than that to define me.
I don't want my moods and my feelings to define me.
I am not dependent on my thoughts and my relationship to others, because who I am is Perfection.
Therefore, I can let go of my concepts, my sins, my expectations.
I can let go of them, look at myself, and say: Here I am, ready to start all over again, ready to continue to create in the Light.
I AM THAT I AM, E'HE'YEH ASHER E'HE'YEH.*
I am a child of the Light, I am Freedom.
I am Perfection. Therefore, everything around me is Perfection.
My whole world is the reflection of who I am.

This is exactly what I want you to do. These are the exact words I want you to use, once you recognize that you are less than free and you desire to be free again. Take these words and turn them into a prayer. Then ask the Light to cut your strings of attachment. I give you this mantra to repeat--I AM THAT I AM, E'HE'YEH ASHER E'HE'YEH. This mantra clothes you in Light. It announces that you are invincible.

I AM THAT I AM is a mantra that states your attunement with the Law. I AM brings forth who you are in an infinite motion. In

---

* Accent the final syllable; pronounce 'e' as in yes and 'a' as in about

Hebrew the form of E'HE'YE makes it even clearer as a process that begins in the now and continues forever. The EH, the Aleph, initiates the creative force of the Presence. Therefore, E'HE'YE ASHER E'HE'YEH leaves no room for the past or for anything that is not in the Light energy of the creation process.

In one moment you can release all the garments you accumulated over eons, by sincerely desiring to be free. Then you can start with a clean slate to create in the Light, and to become who you really are. This is the essence of repentance--not putting your attention on the strings, but desiring to be Light again and starting anew, now. When you do that and truly establish this desire in fullness, you will experience Freedom and joy that you have never known before. With Freedom and joy will come a whole new creation. Then your creation will be free of the strings of attachment and will reflect who you really are. Once you have this experience of being a conscious creator, it will be easy to return again and again to this moment of now, to a new beginning.

*What happens to the physical body, the garment, at death?*

Shedding the body, what you call "death," means letting go of the outer garment, in order to use a lighter garment of your soul. A more advanced level, mentioned in various traditions, is the ability to transform the garment of the body into Light. It is mentioned in the mystical traditions as Merkavah. This is a very highly evolved state of awareness which, at present, only a few are aware of, and even fewer are able to manifest.

*Can we achieve full freedom while in a physical body?*

Yes and no. While being bound in a physical body you can experience Freedom, but not in its purest form, which, by definition, is free of garments.

*And the body is a garment?*

Yes. A human being who understands that the body is just a garment, is freed of attachment to the body. The fear of aging and death, which is the heaviest attachment, is eliminated.

*So we can live in a physical body but still be detached from physicality?*

Indeed. You can achieve high levels of freedom, therefore experience exquisite life while in the body, free of the fear of death. Then, in the process of shedding your body you will fully blossom into Perfection, Freedom.

*What will our daily life be like when we have reached a high level of Freedom?*

Your life will be Life. Various traditions refer to it as the Days of the Messiah, the Golden Age, Heaven on Earth. Heaven on Earth is when the creation is a pure reflection of the Creator, when the subcreations are also a full reflection of the Prime Creator. Heaven on Earth is when every part of Earth, of physicality, is imbued with Perfection. This means there is no room for less than Perfection, for strings of attachment--every one lives by the Law. How would this affect everyday life? Can you imagine a world where there is no anger, where people don't try to control others, where greed is nonexistent?

*Does it mean that every moment in life we as creators need to choose where to put our attention?*

Yes. This is your responsibility as a creator. You have to grow up and take responsibility. People mistake the saying about being 'innocent as a child' to mean being swept away as a child. A child is innocent by virtue of his natural tendency to put attention on bliss. But as you grow up you need to be more conscious about where you put your attention. Don't let others--people, the news, circumstances--tie strings on you, influence you. In this respect, you don't want to be a child who is easily influenced. This is called conscious living. You wouldn't want your Prime Creator to be unconscious while creating you. Why do it to your creations? And don't mistake Me, God did not create imperfections, as some people think. God is all possibilities. It is up to you to choose only Perfection.

September 21, 1996

## 27

## The Glory of the Heart

The heart is the center of your physical life, and as long as it beats you are alive, but your nonphysical heart continues long after your physical existence ends. This Heart is the center of your spiritual body and the seat of your soul. It is the center of your chakra system in all directions, and it is as wide or as narrow as you want it to be. It is your connection to the Source.

The 'breath of Life' moves through your Heart, and it flows to every cell of your body. This breath is more than the supply of oxygen to your cells. This breath is all that you take in, all you 'breathe' through your Heart to your bodies. It is all that you allow to come in. Just as oxygen circulates in the heart and moves to the cells of your body, so the 'breath of Life' you let in, eventually moves through the Heart to reflect on the rest of your being.

The Heart of your being reflects who you are. What is it that makes one person have 'more heart' than another? It is the ability to maintain the flow of life, to let it come in, to let it circulate, and then express itself. It is the ability to let the Heart beat, unconsciously or consciously, with the beat of Creation. It is the ability to give the Heart its rightful place at the center of life. It is the ability to be in touch with the Heart, not only to allow the Heart to express itself, but also to honor it as your master. By honoring your Heart for what it is, you may find yourself falling in love with it. You may find yourself performing a pilgrimage to your Heart, offering what you would offer to any guru, master or spiritual leader. By turning to your Heart, you will always be able to find the forgotten room full of hope, faith, Light and Love.

I am calling on you today to look for this forgotten room, open its windows and doors, let the light shine out and expand, let it overflow. Nourish it from within and without. Make sure that everything you take into your Heart is of the purest quality, because the nourishment you give your Heart will eventually reach all of your being. What you allow from within your Heart to shine out, is a reflection of who you are.

If you suffer from any kind of heart disease, it is an indication of your Heart's strong desire to express itself, to break through the boundaries you put on it. It's an indication of the great desire of your life force, not only to exist, but to expand and grow and express who you are. Find within yourself the constrictions you have placed on your Heart. What are you taking in, that doesn't agree with your Heart? What do you not allow to be expressed? Find the constrictions and dissolve them. Dissolve them not only for the sake of your health, but for the sake of your being.

Your Heart is also the home of your emotions, the emotions that make you so human. You use expressions like, "Oh, it warms my heart," "it breaks my heart," "she has a heart of gold." When you use these expressions you don't mean the four-chambered physical heart that sits in the middle of your lungs. You mean the Heart which is the seat of your soul. If you don't allow your Heart to exist at its best, how do you justify your existence? When you fully express what is in your Heart you allow it to shine forth its Godliness, to choose good, to bring forth kindness, love, forgiveness and grace. An open Heart is an open channel for the grace of God. It is only through the merit of such Hearts that the grace of God is expressed.

The purer the Heart, the more Light comes through; the purer the Heart, the more powerful you are. This probably contradicts what you are accustomed to believing. You associate kind people with weakness. I strongly emphasize, the purer the Heart, the more powerful you are. When your blood is nourished with pure oxygen, all the cells of your body celebrate. When your emotional and spiritual Heart is allowed to circulate the purest qualities, the first to gain will be your intellect--the clarity of your thoughts. The more powerful your Heart, the more powerful your mind will become, and the balance you achieve between the two will bring you greatness.

The mind is nourished by a constant stream of thoughts, self-perpetuating thoughts, fed by your outer world. These thoughts are like food to the mind. Food must be divided, sifted and digested in order to be beneficial to the body. Only the best part remains to benefit the body while the rest is eliminated. The mind can do only so much in the process of digesting thoughts. The mind can grossly divide beneficial from harmful thoughts, but it is your Heart which helps to sift and extract what's good. Only when you sift the stream of thoughts through your refined feelings and emotions, do these thoughts go through the final stages of purification. What's good turns into Light and what's not beneficial remains behind, like a rock. The purer your Heart, the easier it is to turn any thought into Light and let go of the rest. The purer your Heart, the easier it is to identify what's good, what's pure; the easier it is for the Heart to create a balanced relationship with the mind. In this balance, the mind is slowly trained to take in only what the Heart desires. In this way your whole being learns to utilize all its faculties to their utmost potential, to fulfill their original intent, and to reflect the Heart of God.

Every emotion, feeling and thought generated and circulated in your being is legitimate. It is there for a reason. But a healthy system knows how to sift what's beneficial to produce the best results. You can continue to generate 'negative' thoughts--feelings of guilt, hate, envy, judgment. You can feed yourself with whatever your lower desires call you to have. It is legitimate. It is part of you. But is it really the choice you want to make? Is it really what your Heart desires? Does it really make you happy? Does it produce balance in your life?

Why not make a conscious choice now, rather than on your deathbed? It is all in your hands. If you don't know how or where to begin, find this place in your Heart, this forgotten little room full of Light, and ask for more Light. Because no matter how dark life seems to be and how immersed you are in negativity, this small desire of yours is all that is needed. Once you turn your attention to the Flame in your Heart, it will grow and grow like a little flower that is watered. It will attract more of its kind, more Light. And slowly you will find that Light takes over. Then you will find friends that see a different you. You will find events and circumstances that enter your life in a way you never dreamt. You will find that your mind becomes a servant of your Heart, and that your life changes. It is really much simpler than you think. You have to choose. Do it now. I am calling you--find Me now.

Just as I speak through this one today, I speak to you in your Heart. There are no better ones than others. You are all My children. Keep the door open. The Light pours wherever it is allowed to flow. If you want to be counted in the new game, and if you want to be part of the glorious play, keep your door open. Awaken, I am calling you. It is never too late. Look at your Heart and what you will see there is the reflection of your being. Glorify your Heart and what you will see is Glory.

*So this room of Light where the whole universe resides, is in the center of our existence?*

Yes, it's even more than the center. It's a line of Light connecting all the chakras, anchoring you to Earth and to Heaven. The purer and stronger this room becomes, the more tangible it becomes, and the more connected you feel to Light. The saints who radiate Light have this experience. The effulgence radiates in all directions, but it begins in the Heart.

*How can we purify our being and bring Glory to our life, as you invite us to do?*

It is a matter of where you put your attention, what you choose to include in your life, where you are centered, how much you allow the Self to be part of your life.

*How would doing this affect our daily life? How would we start our day differently?*

By taking a minute or two to appreciate everything around you. By giving thanks, smiling, acknowledging other people's smiles and looking for what is good. By sending a child to school with a big hug and a smile, by resolving to talk differently to employees, fellow workers or schoolmates today. Maybe not reading the newspaper this morning. While driving consider slowing down and letting other people pass while they rush to their work. Send flowers to somebody, call your mother, your brother or sister, and say a good word. You know all these things, you just don't take time to stop and do them. But it is much more than doing. It really begins with taking the time for appreciating, for noticing the Light, for acknowledging the goodness. It begins with desiring more love for yourself and others. Look into your Heart in a moment of silence and feel the warmth. Feel the burning Flame that you have inside, get in touch with It.

You don't need to read books. You don't need to understand intellectually. The Flame is right there inside you, let it be expressed, let it be known to you. This I call "opening the door." By doing this a minute or two a day, the Flame will grow and expand in you. You'll extend a hand and I will send armfuls to you. Most important of all, be innocent. Don't expect anything. When you are innocent, and

you let the Silence be expressed in you, you find yourself able to see
the Silence in others. In the midst of annoyance or anger in a busy
day, you will be able to close your eyes for a minute and find this
place inside you that will bring you back to balance immediately. It
will remind you who you really are and why you are here and who
those around you are and why they are here.

All this is not about money, accomplishments, acquisitions or
accumulation of wealth. It is about this dear Silence inside you.
After you acknowledge this master within, and offer It whatever is in
your heart, you can go about your day pursuing your achievements,
your struggle, anything you want to do. When you start from this
place within, your day will be lighter. Therefore I say, by glorifying
your Heart, you glorify all creation. Each one of you count. Each
one of you makes a difference. Appreciate and give tribute to the
burning Flame in your Heart, to the silence of your Heart. Your
Heart will tell you where to go and what to do. By honoring your
Heart you honor Me.

September 24, 1996

## 28

## The Illusion of the Shadows

Have you ever noticed the play of shadows that the leaves of a tree create on the ground, when the sun sends its rays through the branches? If you watched long enough you probably discovered the nature of this play. The shadows move; sometimes they are darker, sometimes lighter. There is no fixed pattern. It is indeed a play, a dance, in which the shadows continue changing in shape, in darkness, in place. All of it depends on the light. The existence of the shadows is an illusion. One moment you see them and the next you don't--there is no stability. A slight movement of a leaf or branch reveals the stability of the light that pours through. If you take away the branch altogether, the shadows disappear. It's fun to watch the play, drawing comfort from the brightness of the light, knowing that without the rays of light, the play couldn't take place.

This is how real the shadows in your life are. Sometimes they appear as all dark in contrast to the light, and sometimes they are different shades, from gray to black. Each shadow derives its characteristics from its surroundings. What might seem black to one person is light gray to another. You observe, absorb and experience the qualities of shadows that prevail in your life in reference to others, always weighing, comparing, and contrasting. You go through life comparing the yesterdays with the present. You compare other people's experiences with your own, looking at their qualities, feelings and thoughts in relation to yours. You draw conclusions in this comparison--what is lighter, what is darker, what is better, what is worse, who is right and who is wrong.

You are like children who focus their gaze on the shadows of the leaves, forgetting altogether that the existence of those shadows depends on the light. Lift your eyes, look at the sun, and the shadows disappear. They were just a play on the ground, an illusion. The shadows you see in your life, that seem so real, are no different. The point where you find your shadows relative to others' is illusory as well. There is only one reference point--absolute Light, Love, Perfection.

Where to begin? How do you step out of the arena of shadows, of relative experience? How can you go to a higher place to observe the play and control it at the same time? How do you find a place where you can choose between this play or another, or remain completely in the Light? This place is inside you. Just as you could move a few steps to view the play of shadows from a different point, you can go within to view the play of your life from a very different point. For this, you first need to want to step out of the play, and to let go of the relativity of the situation. You need to find the will power and strength within. You need to let go of your involvement. You need to stop the busy activity of your mind and your feelings, and observe them from another vantage point. Who is the one who can actively decree silence on this activity? You. You are the only one who can do it. At times you have naturally stopped, and from that place of non-activity you made a decision to follow a certain direction. You have this innate ability.

If you follow your innate ability to step out of the play, you can control the quality of the play, influence it or eliminate it altogether. You are the steady source of Light that plays with the objects to create the dance of shadows. You are the constant Light. Your only reference point is You and your ability to step out of this relativity and observe the play of the shadows. This stepping out is, in fact, stepping in, finding the will power to detach yourself from the play, and to let the Light come all the way through. Then you realize that the shadows were an illusion, that the only Reality, before, during and after the play, is the Light.

Your source of Light is not far away. It's inside you. Light is activated in you naturally when you let it happen, when you stop all action and become still. Observe the process of activity and silence, motion and stillness. Observe yourself being in both places and have the courage to step out of the arena of shadows. Reassess, reevaluate and open up to new possibilities. Then, from stillness, come out and expand to join the game again, this time knowing that its source is Light and Love. From this vantage point you have a better view. You gain the sense of your innate freedom, knowing that you always have the choice to step in or out of the game. You can choose to change the rules, or even begin a new game with new desires, new friendships, new contacts, new knowledge, this time drawing much more bliss from the game.

In order to function well, your systems follow a rhythm of activity and stillness. What you need to realize is that the situations in your life which fluctuate throughout the day, the year, or throughout your life, are like the play of the shadows. Your life is an ongoing cycle of purification, creation, purification, creation. New streams, new ideas, new vantage points, new possibilities and new games. Who plays the games and controls the shadows? Who has the finger on the switch? You. You can choose to infuse the game with Light or you can choose to linger in the shadows and focus on them. As long as you remember that your life flows between these two poles in an ever-spiraling, ongoing flow, you won't stay stuck in the shadows. Choose to join the rhythm of Life, choose to be part of this ever-pulsating, expanding Heart that infuses Light and Love into your life. Then you will experience the bliss that is generated by the rays of Light when they penetrate through the branches to create the patterns on the ground.

*I understand that it is not enough for someone to hear or read about Love and Light. Rather, he himself needs to experience it. Can you please talk about the difference between knowing the Bible and other spiritual literature and experiencing it oneself?*

You can benefit from outside knowledge, such as the Bible, a teacher or friend, when you are ready to receive it. But if you don't prepare the bed of readiness, no matter how much knowledge or information you are given, the experience will never grow. Even if people think that what saved or changed their life is what somebody else told them or showed them, it was initially their own readiness. Such an experience comes only when a person consciously or unconsciously withdraws from outside activity to a place of silence, of rest, of receptivity, to come out in a new direction. Some people go within but do not quite know how to cultivate silence. In a way, they do only half the job. Therefore, they come out into the same reality, and move in the same direction.

A good example of this is your night's sleep. Do you take advantage of your sleep to wake up to a new reality? Or do you wake up to the same old reality? Are you willing to start anew and let the Light and the Love that call you from within shine forth? Or are you still blocking them by thoughts, hesitations, doubts, comparisons, embarrassment, manipulation and overshadowing feelings?

This is a step by step process: you withdraw, you look at what is shadowy in your life, you move it aside and invite the Light. If you follow this process and are receptive to the Light, then a friend's advice, a quote from the Bible, a new idea or new inspiration will assist you to open to a new reality. But if you don't quite remove the shadows, the new idea, knowledge and support won't be expressed fully or may not be expressed at all, and you will perpetuate your overshadowed experience again and again.

*Would you say that at the final stage, when one invites the Light, one needs to be trusting, and maybe bold, too?*

You look the shadow in the eye, you move 'the branch' aside, you open up to the Light. Then boldly and actively create what you want with the new knowledge or feeling that you let shine through you. The only way to do it is by trusting.

*Thank You. If someone takes advantage of others to make money in unfair ways, how can he realize that he is in the shadow? How can he overcome such a challenge?*

Being in the shadow is different than being in the play of shadows. Being in absolute shadow is a hard place to be. There is no contrast, no play. Sometimes it takes a whole lifetime for a person to come out, and sometimes more than that. A person who comes out of absolute shadow is extremely courageous and insightful, drawing only from his inner Light, unveiling what was there in the depth of his Heart. But for most people, who are in the play of shadows, some outside experience evokes the inner Light to express and shine forth. Very few live in absolute darkness. Almost everyone has a chance to find knowledge or an experience that will evoke the inner Light. It could be the smile of a child at the street corner, or the death of a close one, or the advice of a friend. Each person is invigorated by a different kind of experience. Remember, what seems to you to be absolute darkness, is still an illusion. Even people who seem to take advantage of others and promote 'badness' instead of 'goodness,' will find their way to let the constant source of Light hidden inside them, shine forth.

*Fear, hate, jealousy, etc. merely block the Light. The only life-supporting reality is Love and Light. Is this so?*

Indeed. This is not just a saying. This is an everyday experience. You can experiment with it. Examine the 'weight' of love and hate. Research the energy that each draws from you or benefits you. How do you feel when you express anger? What happens to your energy and the energy field around you? How much energy does anger draw from you? How much mending do you have to do later? Then experiment with the opposite. How do you feel when you express love? How easily does love come to you? How much lightness is around you? How many good things happen in your environment? Weigh the two possibilities, calculate, and you will find that love provides you with energy while opposite feelings take energy away from you. You will find that love is more beneficial and that there is no better investment than an investment of Love and Light.

September 29, 1996

## 29

## Make God Your Personal Friend

How do you bring the ever-pulsating Heart to your everyday life and make God your personal Friend? Throughout the book We have been talking about this topic. We approached it from many angles. We offered different ways of looking at the same idea in a variety of fields. We used expressions such as, "turn your face to Me," "love Me as I love you," "see Me in your Heart," "awaken, I am calling you," "desire Me," and others. Now I would like to pin it down to your daily schedule. Everything that will be said are suggestions that can be used in all combinations, partially or completely, as long as the spirit is kept. Many traditions have already been established, known and practiced by millions of people, which strive to achieve the same thing--evoke devotion in the Heart. Some are very detailed and include every aspect of life, every hour of the day, and some are general. They are all wonderful, if you are drawn to practice them joyfully. If you discover resistance within yourself, or if you find that you are following directions mechanically, stop. Rethink what you are doing and why.

What I will suggest here today could fit into any existing practice, or substitute for it, as you wish or choose, as long as you have the understanding that the practice itself is secondary. The only importance of the practice is the intention behind it, and the degree of joy with which it is maintained. It is important only to the degree that it cultivates the quality of devotion, the superiority of your spiritual self over your physical self, thus opening the passage towards the goal. What is the goal? As far as I am concerned the goal in very simple terms is to find Me in your Heart, to make God your personal Friend, Teacher, Lover and Companion. And if you can achieve all this without a practice, good. And if you feel you need help to cultivate it in your Heart, here are My suggestions:

Create a little ceremony, alone, with family members or close friends, in which you set the cornerstone and lay the foundation for an inner temple that you 'build' in your Heart. Get excited, prepare the ceremony as if you were preparing a surprise party. Beautify yourself and your surroundings. You may include any music, prayers, quotations, food--any objects dear to you, according to your tradition. When you are ready say:

I hereby declare that I am prepared to build and maintain a Temple in my Heart for the presence of God to dwell in always.
I hereby declare that in the center of this Temple I light an eternal Flame that will radiate Light and Love, from now to eternity, through my body to my bodies, to the universe.
I hereby declare that I will always remember the eternal Flame and will always turn to It to draw Light and Love for myself and the world.

Remain silent for as long as you need to visualize your Temple and the Flame in its midst, and conclude with the resolution that from now to eternity you have a Home and a Friend; you have a Home and a Mother and a Father waiting for you there; you have a Home and Guidance. You will never be lost again. You always have a Home to turn to, in times of happiness and times of sorrow. Now that you have a Home, you are strong like a rock. There is nothing in the world that can touch your Home or take it away from you.

Here are some small reminders to keep you on track on a daily basis. If you find equivalents to your own tradition in any of the suggestions which follow, by all means keep your tradition. If you don't have any, create your own with your own words. Before you retire to bed for a night's sleep, give thanks for everything that happened throughout the day. Letting go of all that took place during the day, ask for a good night's sleep that will refresh and rejuvenate your body and soul. The simple process of giving thanks helps you let go. But if you find your mind attached to the happenings of the day, and find it hard to fall asleep, make a point of giving each part of your body as an offering to God. Lie on your back, relax, breathe deeply, and then slowly, slowly, starting from your toes, relax each part of your body, offering it to God. Say, "I love you, toes. I now give you back to God." Then relax your ankles and say, "I love you, ankles. I now give you back to God." Then relax your calves and say, "I love you and give you back to God," and so forth until you relax the muscles in your face, your eyes, all the way to the top of your head and you give it all back to God. By this time you will be in deep relaxation, ready to fall asleep if you aren't already asleep. If it doesn't work the first night, don't jump to conclusions. Keep on doing it until your body learns to relax, be at ease and trust the process.

Upon awakening in the morning, sit up in your bed, and give thanks for the night. Then open your eyes, look around you and focus on a few things that you appreciate. Avoid anything that draws your attention in the direction of annoyance. Your appreciation can go to children, spouse, birds singing outside, a picture, a good memory, a flower, a pattern on the rug, the play of the rays that come through the window--anything you want to appreciate. The whole thing doesn't take more than a minute. Now you have your day before you. Whether it is a day of work or study, play or responsibility, a busy day or a free day, it is always a day in which you can live every minute, with your eternal flame, your God within. When you take your Flame wherever you go, you will spread Love and Light in every interaction throughout your day.

If you are inclined to a more spiritual pursuit, set aside another time in the morning, ten to thirty minutes, for going within. You can follow any of the known meditation practices. You can also let your imagination lead you to the Temple inside your Heart. Generate excitement, wholly and completely bring yourself to that Temple, envisioning the Flame, feeling its warmth, enjoying its glory. Envelop yourself with Light and Love. Talk with God--whether for you, in that moment, God is your Teacher, Mother, Father or Inner

Guidance--whatever name you give God, It is your God in your Temple. Talk to God from a place of Love and Light. Ask whatever your Heart desires and give tribute to it. Ask and expect to receive answers.

Withdraw to the Temple and forget all about your outer world. Dwell in your inner world. It is all yours. Within this Light and Love you are absolutely protected. When you come out of your Temple for your daily activity, Light and Love, and your Friend will go with you wherever you go. If, during the day, you happen to forget, you will find your way back Home easily, since it is so familiar. Then the phrase "turn to Me" will become your daily experience. What you see throughout the day will remind you of Home. If what you encounter during the day offers discord, if it feels as if it doesn't belong, gently disregard it. It is not an enemy, it just doesn't belong in your Home. If it keeps on knocking, you can invite it Home, but remember, your Home includes only Love and Light. You cannot bring in shadows.

Therefore, before opening the door you have to learn to forgive, to accept, to give and receive, to learn to include rather than resist. Then whatever you open your door to, turns into Love and Light in your experience. The shadows are begging to be included in your Home, which is full of Light and Love. They don't want to be left out. You have the power to transmute them into Light and Love, whether they are self issues, that have to do with your physical, emotional or mental body, or issues that concern your family, your friends, your work place, etc. And even if a worldwide issue troubles you, you can illumine it from your own perspective, with your own Love and Light and let it come into your Temple so it won't trouble you any more.

Remember, you are the ruler in your kingdom. You are the one at Home, safeguarded, illumined by Love and Light. You are the one who decides whether or not to open the door. You are the one who can grant forgiveness and acceptance to yourself and others.

These suggestions are not to be taken lightly. The Temple in your Heart, the burning Flame in your Heart, are tangible and real. What is not tangible and what is not real, is your ignorance of them, your neglect in recognizing their existence. By once again inviting them into your life, you will only gain. God, who 'used to be' in heaven or in books, will return to His rightful place in your Heart to be your 'personal' God, as a very tangible experience in your life.

And from this place, everything else that was described and explained in this book will gain a new perspective. The burning Flame in your Heart will illumine every aspect of your life. Issues of life and death, of health, business, education, politics, relationships, personal crisis, will all be seen in a different light. The realities in which you fixed yourself will shift, and your life will have a Godly quality. When you carry God in your Heart, everyone you meet will naturally carry their own Flame--God in their Heart--and any need for judgment, comparison, control is eliminated. There is only one God, there is not one God that is better than another. If the one God is called by different names in different religions and atheism, this is just the play of diversity. The Flame is burning. Light and Love are eternal, are one.

*If after establishing theTemple in the Heart, one meets a rough situation in life where love is not apparent, how would You encourage the person to go on even though there are obvious challenges?*

For this you have the daily routine of thanks upon retiring and rising in the morning to remind you of your connectedness to the beauty of life. I recommend a period of time in which, on a regular basis, you visit your Heart, your temple, to tend to the Flame, to communicate with the Flame. In your communication with the

Flame, you can ask It to burn away unpleasant encounters, unpleasant attachments, situations. During the encounter, since the Flame is already so well established in your Heart, just lightly touch your heart chakra, knock at the door of your own Temple, remind yourself that what you see out there is just an illusion, a shadow. No matter how tangible the illusion seems, the Flame is the eternal reality.

*During this encounter, can you ask your Heart how to handle the situation? Is there any way to receive specific guidance in such situations?*

Definitely. Touch your heart chakra lightly and say, in your own words, "God, please help me. Please handle the situation for me." Take a deep breath, and let whatever comes through you handle the situation. If what you observe coming through you is again anger, resistance or violence, reassess. Close your eyes and start the process again, saying, "God, please help me. Handle the situation for me." Then observe what comes through you this time; until you unveil, until you pave the way for your inner Light and Love to come through and illumine the shadows.

Remember, *you* have to let Light and Love come through. You have to open the door for them to express and do their work. It's an in and out, in and out process. The only one who can open or close the door is you. If you find yourself overshadowed by fear, anger, depression, then you know that you are keeping your door closed to the Light. As We said before, look at the shadow, recognize it for what it is and then open the door. The shadow cannot withstand Love and Light. It disappears, saturated by Love and Light, transmuted.

October 1, 1996

181

## 30

## Awaken, Children of the Light

Dear children of the Light.
The day is coming for your full potential to take its rightful
    place.
Your essence is Light and Love enabling you to flow
    in the ever-expanding stream of Life.
Your image and likeness is Divine.
Your image and likeness is carried within the Self
    and it is all you needed or will ever need to be perfect.
You are children of the Light.
Creation is the story of Light.
Therefore, what Is, is Light.
Light is like an invisible woven thread that makes up the
    fabric of what Is.
Even the gaps between the threads are included in the fabric.
You don't say, "Only the threads of the fabric are my blanket,
    and what's in between the threads is not my blanket."
The same goes for Creation.
Like a warm blanket, Creation cradles you, protects you,
    provides you with all you need to come forth
    with your own special uniqueness,
    knowing at all times that you are protected.
You are the children of the Light, children of God--El.
Therefore, I am calling you today to take your rightful share
    in this Creation.
The legacy is yours, waiting for you to awaken to all its
    promised possibilities.
The blanket of Light is tingling.
Awaken from your slumber.
Rise, open your hearts and let your inner Light shine through,
    merging with the infinite Light all around you.

Don't let the shadows deceive you.

They are but illusions that have taken hold in your life for far too long, so long that you even embroidered them into your blanket, believing that the shadows add to the beauty of the fabric of your life.

Time to undo this embroidery.

Light is infinite beauty.

Accept your rightful share and be who you really are--

Children of the Light.

October 3, 1996

# Epilogue

## Tomorrow is a Day of Awakening

Tomorrow spring begins.
Tomorrow is a day of awakening, the beginning of a new era
in human history.
Tomorrow is when all the souls that have chosen to be on
earth in this time, will come together as one big Soul and
acknowledge their connection to each other and to the
source.
Tomorrow is when the excitement of one pure soul will send
forth vibrations that will touch each and every soul and
awaken it to fully experience the freshness of the moment.
Tomorrow is when all the waves will meet the shore in one
big hum of praise to the Lord and the soul of every man,
woman and child will hear this hum and awaken into a
glorious, bright and warm spring day.
Tomorrow the birds will chirp and the sun will send her
warm rays and the wind will blow its gentle breeze and it
will be just as beautiful as now.
A wave of excitement will run through all hearts and
announce the coming of that tomorrow.
Tomorrow will be the Awakening.
Then, your inner eyes will open and you will look at each
other and see God in everyone.
Your inner ears will hear the glorious song of Creation.
The waves in your heart will break with joy against the shore
of your existence and wash away all sorrows.
Tomorrow you will all stop for a fraction of a moment and
join the big hum--Aum Selah.

March 20, 1996

# Appendix

*Many people look at channeling as some strange metaphysical and esoteric phenomenon when, in actuality, there is not a person in this world who does not channel all the time. Everyone is a channel; the key point is who or what is being channeled...As you gain mastery over your energies you develop total control of what you channel. The ideal is to become a channel for those energies that serve the soul and God.*

Joshua David Stone, Ph.D. author of
*Soul Psychology* and *The Complete Ascension Manual*

## Guidelines for conversing with God

I developed these guidelines together with my dear friend. You can follow these guidelines or later develop your own.

1. Always make sure that you are surrounded by Love and Light and are conversing with the Highest. Use the name "God" or other name of God at the start of each question. You might say out loud or inwardly, "I now attune myself to the Source of All Knowing, or, I would like to access the Source of All Knowing and receive God's love and light."
2. Be relaxed and well rested.
3. Drink water before and during the communication. Water increases the conductivity of electricity in the body.
4. Put the palm of your hand on the center of your chest. Press with the other hand to create close contact between the center of the palm and the chest. This helps to shift your attention from the intellect to the heart.
5. Be clear about your desire to converse with God. Be innocent and trust the process.
6. Mentally ask your intellect to step aside and let you become like a pure vessel for God's knowledge.
7. Wait for inner silence and peace. Put your attention/awareness into the center of your chest, dive into your heart and 'hear...'

## Other Points

You will not hear a voice. What you 'hear' is an inner knowing. I call it, "A thought that is not my own." Play with it until you can tell whether God is talking to you or you are talking to yourself. After some practice, you will be able to tell the difference. Of course there is no way to know ahead of time what you'll first hear, but chances are that it will be words of love. Don't try to remember or analyze what you are hearing, but rather allow it to flow freely. You might want to record the message on tape.

Now for your questions to God: you want to articulate your question and be clear regarding what you want to know. Focus on one topic at a time, and be clear in your intention. It is a good idea to write down your questions and what you desire to know.

Remember, the answers are given to you from the Divine perspective in which everything is part of your growing experience. For example, if you ask, "Is it good for me to do so and so?" the answer may be "yes", having a different meaning comparing to what you consider "good" to be. If you ask questions about time, ask for Earth time. Do not use the word "soon," it is too vague. Do not ask a question with the word "should" in it. Do something because you desire to do it, not because you feel you should do it. You might ask, "Would it be in my highest and best interest to..."

The answers you receive are for the _now_ until a new awareness comes and a new now is created. Divine answers promote Free Will and do not interfere with your or anybody else's Free Will.

It is a good idea at first to give all your questions about an issue to another person. Then, dive within and being totally unattached, let the other person ask God your questions, allowing the answers to come through you. You might want to consider having your first conversations while sitting down in a comfortable and quiet place. Later on, you can ask questions while walking or performing simple tasks.

God says, "When you come to talk to me, leave the ego at home." Ego means both pride (puffed up ego) and shyness (not knowing

186

your fullness.) Be open to learning. Be open to hearing the answer. Be ready to receive the Truth. It is a good idea to repeat what you have learned from God at the end of an answer. Then ask, "Is this correct?" In this way it gives God a chance to hear what you learned and correct any misunderstanding. Also ask, "Do I need to know more now?" or "What else do I need to know now?" It says that you are in a state of surrender, open enough to what you need to know.

In your relationship with God, you can have whatever you want/need--Father, Mother, Friend, Teacher, Lover--all are acceptable. This relationship can change at any moment. You can call for the relationship that you desire. However, you may get the relationship you need.

Be on the watch for the intellect getting involved. You may receive wrong answers because of "wishful thinking." You may desire something so much that you get the answer that you want to hear. Desire can color the answer if we do not trust and are not fully connected. As you let go more and more, you will receive the "real thing."

Conversing with God is a purifying experience. You might find that it tires your physiology. Each physiology is different. You might need to rest, take a hot bath or walk more frequently. If, after a while, you find that you cannot "do it", it is because you are purifying. When this happens, be patient and say out loud, so the physiology can hear it, "Thank you God. I know that You are at work within." This will take the sting out of not being able to access Him directly.

In addition, I'd like to share with you what I have received about demanding God's attention. I used to think that it was rude and disrespectful to demand His attention. I thought that I should approach Him as if I were the smallest; He being the largest! But, He tells me that the word "demand" is quite appropriate. It says to Him that you are indeed sure that He exists, and you are indeed sure that you are ready for His attention. Say to God, "I need You and I want You fully in my life, now! I insist on Your presence! I can no longer do without." Remember that you can turn to Him/Her all the time, as much as you wish.

Often, at their first attempt to converse with God, people will have one of these kinds of experiences:

a) Instead of talking directly to you, God may give you an experience. It may be an experience of deep silence, tingling or other experience. Each person has his/her own. This experience may change as you sit and watch. Or, you may access the Source of All Knowing and each time get the same experience. It may be that you need a repetition of this experience until you are able to go on to another. It is highly individual--as all experiences are.

b) You may "see" a picture, light or have a vision of something. Again, it is completely individual.

When either of these experiences happen, rather than the answer to the question that you asked, the following explanation was given: "I want to remind you that there is a higher Truth; that the context of the specific situation is as nothing compared with the importance of knowing/experiencing that Truth. When I can hold before you the vision of the possibilities; when you can perceive that it is within your own experience and within your own ability to access Me/Self/Absolute, then I can begin the unfoldment of your true connection with Me."

God says: "I love you absolutely, fully, truly, no matter whether or not you know it. You don't need to deserve it. You are already fully loved." And, "Play the game, dear ones. It is not hard. It is fun. See this life as a marvelous game, whose simplicity and enjoyment is found in playing the game with Me. And above all, be easy. Ease facilitates the flow of the universe through you. Take it easy, with ease, and offer yourself to Me, allowing Me to be the doer in all that is to be done. Watch and see how effortless all activities become when your hands are Mine, your heart is Mine and your mind is Mine. It only needs from you, your surrender. Dive into silence, having the intent to let go, and then proceed into action. Remember, I am already you--it only needs for you (self) to let go and recognize that God (Self) does a far better job at living life!"

**Personal Readings with the Author;**
**God Speaks Newsletter and Study Groups**

* Personal readings with Dorit Har are available in person or via the telephone, or through the mail, accompanied by an audio recording.

* A God Speaks Newsletter and Study Groups are planned to start at the beginning of 1999. If you would like to subscribe to the newsletter, lead or participate in a study group in your area, please write to the author.

For more information:

Dorit Har
P.O. Box 11261
Boulder, CO 80301
dmlhar@bouldernews.infi.net
dmlhar@hotmail.com